C
the
God Code

MICHAEL SAWARD

MOWBRAY

For
my godchildren
Michael,
Rebecca and
Fiona

Mowbray
A Cassell imprint
Artillery House, Artillery Row
London SW1P 1RT

First published 1974 by
Scripture Union as *Don't Miss the Party*
Revised edition first published by Mowbray 1989

British Library Cataloguing in Publication Data
Saward, Michael
   Cracking the God code. – Rev. ed.
   1. Church of England. Christian doctrine
   I. Title
   230'.3

ISBN 0–264–67169–4

Typesetting by Chapterhouse, The Cloisters, Formby
Printed and bound in Great Britain by Cox and Wyman Ltd,
Reading

FOREWORD

The 'God-code' needs cracking for most
young people and the content of
Michael Saward's book certainly
cracks it.

Michael Saward's way of expressing
things is fresh and free from jargon.
The book sparkles. A book like this is
needed today.

MICHAEL A. BAUGHEN
Bishop of Chester

CONTENTS

Cracking
the
God-code

ALL over France, ears were pinned to radio sets as the voice droned on monotonously. 'The chiropodist is ticklish. The raven croaks. The cranes are flying. The verdigris is cold' and so on. Just a meaningless jumble of senseless phrases? Not a bit of it. To those who knew the code it all made very good sense. In 1944 a single phrase—the right phrase—could set a huge operation going, disrupting roads, railways, telephones, indeed everything that could assist the coming invasion of France.

The very idea of codes, of secret messages, is great fun. Children love to make their own codes up and feel 'in the know' while others puzzle to understand what all those disconnected letters and numbers mean. Of course it stops being fun when the codes are all part of deadly serious espionage and hundreds, perhaps thousands, of lives are at stake.

To many people the Christian religion is a kind of code. It's all a matter of words and symbols which the ordinary person just doesn't understand. Apparently the religious people enjoy

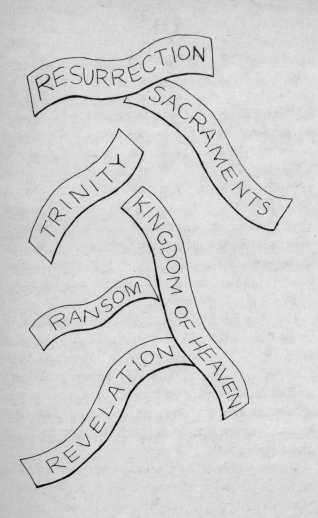

2

using the code and bounce quite meaningless words back and forward among themselves but nobody else has a clue what it means.

So this book is an attempt to crack the God-code and to use, as far as possible, ordinary words to explain what it's all about. It isn't, let's be honest, completely possible to succeed because some technical words are needed in all walks of life. How would a mechanic get on if he couldn't call a carburettor by its actual name?

NO SECRET

It's true that Christianity is greatly concerned with cracking the code. As St Paul put it, the 'mystery' has been revealed. It isn't a secret any more. The code has *been* cracked. But, of course, there's much more to Christianity than simply knowing the essential religious answers.

Christians are people who are on their way to a party—the most fabulous party ever. Now everyone loves a good party. Everyone looks forward to it—young and old alike. So let's start cracking the code and putting on our party clothes. Both ideas are exciting on their own. Together they make an unbeatable combination.

Someone up there...?

SOONER or later everyone has to decide whether there really is a Someone up there. From the very beginnings of time people have always thought there was, but lately the rumour has got around that either there never was anyone or that, if there was, he has recently died off. Some people say that modern science has shown that belief in God (or whatever you call the Someone) is just a load of superstition.

The first Russian astronaut actually said that he'd been out in space and never caught a glance of any Great Someone, Somewhere so obviously it was all a pack of lies. I even met a woman once who was sure that God must be angry with the Apollo moonshots, because it was all wrong for men to go trespassing in God's back garden and that we ought to stay put here on earth where God had put us!

CANNIBAL

Aren't some people stupid? Just suppose I said to my wife 'Darling, you're so gorgeous I could eat you' and she ran out in the street screaming that

4

I'd turned cannibal. Well, wouldn't most people say 'You stupid woman, don't you know the difference between picture-language and literal, scientific language?' Of course they would. So isn't it strange to think that so-called intelligent men and women can actually think that there isn't a Someone because an unbelieving Russian astronaut couldn't find one when he was in orbit. Don't tell me that you believe the hymn-writer actually meant that God was just out of sight when he wrote 'there's a Friend for little children above the bright blue sky'.

All right. We have to use a kind of poetic language when we talk about the Someone. But that doesn't mean we are simply making it all up. It's true that no-one can actually prove that there is a God but then it's also true that no-one can prove that there isn't. Some people go on to say 'Well, if you can't prove it either way I'm not taking sides. I'm going to call myself an agnostic.' It always amuses me to think that 'agnostic' is a Greek word which has the same meaning as the Latin word 'ignoramus' and the English word 'clue-less'.

PROVE IT!

But must we avoid taking sides? Suppose you say to your wife 'I love you' and she says 'You can't prove it, can you?' the fact is you *can't*. You can be kind to her, say nice things about her, give her presents, sleep with her—but that doesn't *prove* that you love her. Nor does it prove that you *don't*. Which only goes to show that nobody has ever been able to prove or disprove a claim to love or be loved. But that hasn't stopped millions of people from believing it. And why is that? Simply because the evidence—such as it was—seemed to be pretty heavily on one side. But they couldn't prove it!

Now I certainly can't prove that there is a Someone called God. But I do think that the evidence leans heavily that way. See if you can follow my line of reasoning...

Here I am looking at the world around me. If I am going to be a contented pig with my snout in the trough, grubbing for my materialistic comforts, then obviously I shan't look around me, except greedily, and I certainly won't look up. So who wants to be a pig? Millions of people seem prepared to settle for lives of grunting piggery. But suppose I'm not content to be a pig? I shall have to start asking real questions and the answers will be vitally important.

QUESTIONS

Now here's the first question. As I look at the universe all around me, I want to know whether it has any meaning. Is it all utterly pointless or can some meaning be discovered? In practice I have to make my mind up one way or the other. Most people find it hard to accept that nothing has any meaning. They act on the assumption that life *does* have some meaning.

Second question: is it rational or totally lacking in any kind of order? Most people seem to be able to find some sort of reasonableness. The universe isn't totally chaotic. There appear to be laws at work in nature. Most of us rely on that assumption.

On to number three. Can I distinguish any kind of purpose about it all? Do things seem to be merely going from nowhere to nowhere or is it all leading towards something? Most people think it is.

Point four: most people see the highest human virtue as sacrificial love. Self-giving that goes on giving. So where did that spring from? Is there love at the heart of the universe? Or did it just evolve? If so, how come, since 'survival of the fittest' seems to suggest that the most ruthless are the winners. Wouldn't that 'breed out' love pretty quickly? Take your pick.

Number five concerns justice. Is there any justice to be had or will the thugs always win? Is goodness rewarded or is honesty merely a mug's game? When a small boy yells out 'It's not fair', he's showing a deep sense of how wrong things can be. So will they ever be put right? How? And by whom?

All of which brings me to the point of saying that every one of us has to come to some conclusions. Either there is, at the very heart of the universe, meaning—rational, purposeful, just and loving meaning. Or there is not. And if there is irrational, unjust, purposeless, hateful nothingness then God help us all. Except that there isn't a God.

One more thing. Which is the higher form of life—a tree or a human being? Naturally you say, 'a human being'. Or to put it another way, 'personality'. So why do some people say they believe in a Force rather than a Person. Surely because they confuse the idea of a Personality with that of a human body. But by personality we mean Life as opposed to existence.

GOD

So what Christians believe is that the evidence of our world points to a Rational, Meaningful, Purposeful, Just and Loving Personality at the heart of the Universe. We can't *prove* him or *disprove* him. But we think the evidence for, is better than that against. And we call him 'God'. A Someone—not just a Something.

By the way, when I say 'him' I'm not being sexist. That's the pronoun Christians use, following the Bible. It doesn't mean that they think God is endowed with masculine appendages!

Just suppose that it's true. That there really is

Someone at the heart of it all. Think of the consequences. It means for sure that everything that
exists can only exist because he exists—he holds
it all together. It means that he started it all
off—that he upholds it and that goodness will
ultimately come out on top.

And what excites Christians is that following
such a line of reasoning, based on their observa-
tions of the world as they know it, brings them to
conclusions which tie up exactly with what the
Bible has to say about God.

Take for example these words from a letter
written by Paul, one of the most famous of the
early Christians. Writing to Christians living in
Rome he says:

> **'All that may be known of God by man lies
> plain before their eyes; indeed God himself
> has disclosed it to them. His invisible attri-
> butes, that is to say his everlasting power
> and deity, have been visible, ever since the
> world began, to the eye of reason, in the
> things that he has made.'***

REASON

You notice Paul doesn't say 'visible to the eye of
faith'. He says 'visible to the eye of reason'. In
other words the existence of God makes sense.
Or, to put it another way, if there is no God then
all is non-sense.

*Romans 1.19–20

De-coding nonsense is a terrible waste of time so if you are quite sure there isn't a God then I suggest you throw this book away and start doing something else right now.

Still open-minded? Try reading on.

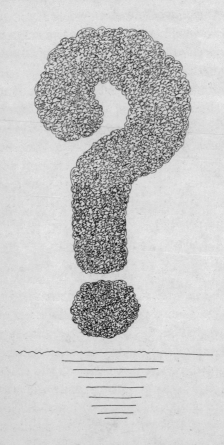

All you
need
is love?

BACK in the nineteen-sixties the Beatles swept round the world on the surge of emotion created by the words: 'All you need is love'. And where did it get them? Well, it certainly brought them fame and money. No doubt about that. But it also taught them some hard lessons. For one thing it taught them that you don't only need love—you also need a good lawyer and a good accountant. Paul McCartney was honest enough to admit that 'We're all talking about peace and love but we're not really feeling peaceful at all'. What happened to the Beatles was living proof that love is *not* all you need.

LAWS

Now don't get me wrong. No Christian is going to say that love is unimportant. But he is going to ask where it comes from and what it means. What's more, he's bound to wonder whether a universe which seems to stick to the rules (what we call the laws of nature) may not also have built into it *moral* laws as well as *scientific ones*.

Look at it this way. Suppose I decide to drive

my car down the wrong side of the road. The law of the land makes it plain that you have to stick to your own side of the road and I'm not ignorant of that fact. But today I feel brim full of love towards the world, and doesn't the song say 'All you need is love'? The result is rather like one of those old Hollywood silent movies—Mack Sennett, wasn't it?—with cars crashing all over the place while I drive merrily on, loving everyone in sight. And, as they pick me out of the smoking wreckage, my last words are, 'I love everybody'.

So there must be some rules. Love isn't the opposite to rules. **Love is playing by the rules, with care for others as you do so. And love is also going on caring for the people who break the rules**.

DEATH TO JIMMY BROWN

So who makes the rules? Some people say that 'doing your own thing' is the way mature adults should behave. But what happens if what I want to do is the opposite to what everyone else wants. To take an extreme case—suppose I hate Jimmy Brown's guts. Frankly, I think the world would be a better place if Jimmy Brown were dead. So, if I follow the 'do-your-own thing' idea of living, all I need to do is pick up a gun and put a stop to Jimmy Brown's career. And why not? Jimmy and his friends should learn to be tolerant people so they must just tolerate my desire to kill Jimmy.

Well, no society can run like that. So, all down through human history, men have made laws. You mustn't kill people. You mustn't steal other people's property. You mustn't run off with the man-next-door's wife or the woman-across-the-road's husband. You mustn't drive motor-cars on the wrong side of the road. And, because somebody has to see that the laws are properly kept, you mustn't punch policemen in the eye. It all helps to make life run more smoothly for the rest of us if everyone keeps the law.

Now, of course, this kind of law—the law which human societies have framed—may be nothing more than the rules which the majority have made. Lots of laws are like that. In a democracy, laws are, by and large, only the reflection of what most people want at any given time. In some democracies it is even possible to make laws which only a minority want. For example, in Britain the death penalty for murder has been abolished by Parliament. Even so, a quarter of a century later, opinion polls continue to show that the majority of people are still in favour of the death penalty. So how do the abolitionists defend their action? The death penalty, they say, is wrong!

EATING PEOPLE

What they mean is that, in some way, there is

something over and above the law, which determines the way we look at certain actions. Do you know that Flanders and Swann song about the young cannibal who shocked his parents by refusing to eat human flesh. 'Eating people is wrong,' he said. They couldn't begin to understand him because their society didn't object to it. They had no laws against it.

So we do recognize that there are things that seem to be, in themselves, wrong. But how do we know? Argue as cleverly as you will, there isn't any logical answer to that unless you believe that there are, built into the way our Universe works, certain things, certain actions, and certain attitudes which are—to put it another way—out of tune with the Universe.

Which is exactly what Christians mean when they say that at the heart of it all there is Someone—God—who has built into the Universe and, more especially, into man's conscience, such things as Right and Wrong. **Christians believe that there are such things as Truth and Falsehood, Good and Evil, Justice and Injustice and that it is God's purpose that men and women should choose to act justly, rightly, truthfully and well.** Many of the Old Testament laws about the ordering of everyday life are followed by the phrase, 'You shall be holy, as I, the Lord your God, am holy'. Which is only another way of saying that moral behaviour comes out of the very nature of God himself.

NO TRUTH

All of which means that if you reject the idea of
God (or even if you won't commit yourself one
way or the other) then you are logically bound to
deny that there *can* be any real truth or goodness. Everything becomes, as the smart-alicks
say, 'relative'. And that means that truth is
debased into nothing more than what some
individual, or what the Party, wants. In Russia,
they keep re-writing their history books to fit into
their latest political viewpoint. What *actually*
happened is less important than what the Party
leaders want people to believe happened.
Hollywood made films in exactly the same way.
And Truth is dead.

But suppose there *is* a God. And suppose he has
made the Universe and does uphold it. (Which
means, incidentally, that the whole thing would
vanish just like that if he changed his mind.) And
suppose that he has made moral laws for mankind's good. What it means is that to disobey
those laws is to act against my own real interests,
to act against other people's interests, to act
against the interests of the whole of mankind, to
act out of harmony with the whole universe, to
act against the eternal purposes of God. My
seemingly unimportant little misdeed (or my un-
willingness to do something which I ought to

have done) is just one more grain of evil on the huge pile of human wickedness.

MISSING–FALLING–CROSSING

Christians have learnt to call it 'sin'. There are various words in the Bible for 'sin'. One means 'missing the mark'. Another means 'falling short'. A third means 'crossing the line'.

When the Beatles sang 'All you need is love' and (whether on purpose or not, I don't know) kidded a whole generation into thinking that a vague desire to be nice to people was all that mankind needed, they couldn't know that within a few years they would be at loggerheads with each other in the law courts. They simply hadn't been realistic enough to acknowledge that the human heart is sinful. We miss the mark, we cross the line, we fall short virtually every day of our lives. **The apostle Paul once put it this way: 'all alike have sinned and are deprived of the divine splendour'.**

But if we do this and if there is a God who made us and sustains us and has a good purpose for us and has built his laws into the universe, won't we have to be answerable one day?

Try wriggling out of that one.

It ain't necessarily so!

SAMMY Davies Jnr echoed the attitude of millions of people when he sang those words—'It ain't necessarily so!'—with a cynical sneer. Did the things recorded in the Bible *really* happen? Can you believe in miracles? Maybe it's all lies, dished up to keep primitive people ignorant?

Let's take stock. Our own reason tells us that it is at least possible that there is a Someone at the heart of our universe. That Someone would need to be the Creator of everything. He would need to be the one who undergirds things, who holds everything together. He would need to be just, loving, a reasonable Being. He would need to be good, the very source of goodness, the fountain of truth.

GALAXIES

Just suppose he really does exist. It wouldn't make one jot of difference one way or the other. Not, that is, unless he could get through to us. Patrick Moore, the astronomer, has said on TV that he believes that there are other civilizations like ours, far away in the galaxies of the universe. He may be right. He may be wrong. But the result is still the same. We have no contact with them and they have none with us. So for all practical purposes they might just as well not be there. It looks like this:

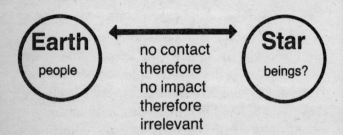

With God, on the other hand, things are different. If he really does exist as Creator and Sustainer then he must be in continuous contact with all that he has made. If he is the Life-giver then he is in contact with all life. If he is the source of all Reason, then he must be in contact with all rational activity. If he is the source of Love, then he must be at the root of all true loving. So the great Someone can be contacted. He can be known. He isn't, in other words, the great No-one. And if he has a purpose for the universe it would not be surprising for him to share it in some way with his rational creatures—men and women.

We could put it in a diagram this way:

GOD

In all things and
beyond all things

people

From that you can see that God, if he is in and beyond everything, must be both at work in mankind and also utterly beyond mankind as well.

Now we human beings can react to things in two ways. We call them our reason and our emotions. Our emotions help us to feel things which we can't always logically explain. As we've already seen we can feel ourselves to be in love, or loved, but we can't rationally prove it one way or the other. When a young couple are about to get married, we should expect them to have used their reason in order to decide whether to take the plunge or not. We should certainly expect them to feel deeply about each other (that's their emotions). But when they come to take the wedding vows they are going beyond reason and emotion into the realm of trust. You could call it an act of faith.

So, we can decide to act in a particular way because our reason tells us to do so. Or we can do it because our emotions urge us to do so. Or we can act because both reason and emotion agree.

GRANDADDY

But we could still be wrong. Suppose I come to the conclusion, after careful thought, that the Universe is ordered and ruled by an old man with a long white beard. I decide to give him a name and I call him 'God'. My reason suggests that such a being is possible. Emotionally, I need a father-figure to give me security. So my reasoning and my feeling assures me that Old Grandaddy God is up there keeping a watchful eye on things. I have a picture of him in my mind and he seems nice and kind and fatherly. I like him.

My friend Tom, however, has quite a different idea. The world to him seems a vicious place, full of greed and violence and the rule of the toughest. So his reason and feelings help to create a mental picture of a universe ruled by a vicious baboon. It makes sense to Tom.

All imagination? Yes, mostly, and neither Tom nor I have any *real* knowledge that there actually *is* a God at all. In a sense, his baboon-god and my grandaddy-god are both no more than inventions of our own fevered imaginations.

INTO ORBIT

Does that mean, then, that the idea of God is nothing more than our thoughts fired off into orbit? Certainly, if we only had our reason and our feelings to go by, that would probably be true. Which is why anyone who relies entirely on feelings and reason alone cannot have a true picture of God (if there is one). I know lots of people whose religious ideas are very largely based on the phrases 'Well, I think ...' or 'Yes, but I feel ...'

All of which only goes to show that unless that Someone, utterly beyond us, makes the effort to get in touch with us somehow, then we are absolutely in the dark.

Suppose then, for the moment, that here I am, an ordinary sort of human being. My mind tells me that it is not unreasonable to believe in a Someone (even though I can well imagine that maybe there isn't one after all). My emotions seem to sense a need for the security and purpose which such a Someone would give (even though I know that my feelings could well lead me astray). Can I ever be sure which is right?

The answer to that is both 'no' and 'yes'. If I am going solely to rely on my mind and my emotions then, 'It ain't necessarily so'. But if the Someone really can communicate with me, than at least I'm on the right road.

Which means that the Someone must, to

use the term the theologians use, 'reveal' himself. There must be a 'revelation' by the Someone. And if there really *is* a revelation then that, and that alone, is going to be the Truth and only a fool would ignore it.

Fasten your seat-belts, we're going on a world tour!

In
search of
a voice

HAS the great Someone ever opened his mouth?
Has he ever broadcast on the human wave-
length? Round the world we go in search of a
voice.

First stop, primitive tribal man. Any sign of a
great Someone with something to say? Well, says
primitive man, our fathers say that there is a
great One far, far away. But we do not know him.
He never speaks with us. What we know is that
there are many spirits who need to be appeased
with offerings. So we make our sacrifices to keep
the spirits happy.

ON TOUR

Not much help there. Off we go again to the East.
To India, to be precise. Hinduism is perhaps the
hardest of all the great world religions to grasp
simply, because it takes on so many different
shapes and faces. Certainly much of the day-to-
day Hinduism of the simple peasant is based on
no more than a series of myths about monkey-
gods and fish-gods, while the cultured academic
philosophy of the educated Hindu is largely a

matter of speculation about the illusory nature of our world. Even those Hindus who believe in some kind of personalized idea of God would never dream of bothering themselves about whether such a God was involved in human history. For them, Jesus or Krishna or anyone else—historical or mythological—can turn out to be some kind of divine expression but his words have no final authority or significance. No voice to be had in Hinduism.

Try Buddhism. Gautama, the founder, certainly bequeathed a philosophy of 'enlightenment' which is rooted in the idea that suffering is at the heart of everything and due to our attachment to the material world. Enlightenment eventually comes to those who reject this life and drop out. But Gautama never claimed to be more than a philosopher and Buddhism is virtually atheistic. If there's no Someone, then it can't be his voice speaking in Buddhism.

How about the old Chinese religions? 'Confucius he say' and so on? Well, Confucius was undoubtedly a wise old man whose proverbs have stood the test of time, but he was never fool enough to think that he was anything more than a philosopher.

NO VOICE

Search high and low in the East, but no one claims to speak for God, other than as a prophet.

24

To most men in the East the very idea of a personal God is meaningless. Their interest lies in
reflecting upon existence and how to cope with it
or deny it.

Let's come further westwards. The great
dominant religion of the Middle East and the
Arab world for over 1300 years has been the
religion of Islam. Mohammed had a series of
visions, in which there was revealed to him the
words of prophecy which have since been called
the Koran (or Quran). Mohammed was probably
unable to read or write, and the words which he
spoke were doubtless remembered and later
written down. But he himself was quite certain
that he was no more than God's prophet. 'God,'
said Mohammed, 'has no partner.'

Here then we get a real claim that God has
spoken. We must come back to it in a moment.
But before we do we must look at the last of the
great ancient religions—Judaism.

**The early history of the Jews is to be found
in the Old Testament and the voice of God, it
is claimed, was heard many times. Person
after person in the story of the Jews heard
'the voice of the Lord'.** Abraham, Isaac, Jacob,
the prophets, the kings and, perhaps, supremely,
Moses. To all these the voice of God came. Yet
none claimed to be more than a prophet, a
mouthpiece.

DIFFERENT

Only when we come to the man called Jesus are we suddenly thrust into a totally different world. Before him there were philosophers and prophets. None claimed actually to be 'one with God'. To Jesus alone we are forced to turn.

If he was wrong, mistaken, deluded, mad, then we need not bother to waste time on him. For one thing is clear. He never claimed to be in the same league as all the rest. He never contented himself with being simply a prophet, a teacher, a philosopher. He and he alone made the greatest, the final claim of all. So if that was not true he was the biggest liar the world has ever known. A thoroughly bad man or a thoroughly mad man. Those are the terms on which he was to be judged—bad, mad, or God.

For such a claim to be made by a Jew was, of course, the most terrible of all blasphemies. Nothing—absolutely nothing—could compare with it. Such a vile deceiver must be destroyed, said the Jewish religious leaders.

The trouble was that while Jesus appears to have made the most outrageous claims, unlike most bad or mad men he backed them up by his actions. **He did everything the Messiah was supposed to do, according to the ancient Jewish prophecies in the Old Testament. He did heal the sick and lame, he did bring sight to the blind, he did raise the dead. And,**

finally, of course, he seems to have broken death's power for himself.

TRUE

Now if this is true,* it has the following effects. First it places him in a totally distinct category from all who had gone before. Thus he fulfilled the truths (and rejected the errors) in the earlier religions. He was not setting up another religion. He was bringing the very truth itself.

But what about Islam, the religion of Mohammed? That, after all, didn't appear on the scene until 600 years *after* Jesus Christ.

Well, we have to say this. If what Jesus taught was true, if he was one with God, if he did rise from the dead then Mohammed, who denied much or all of this, was wrong and a false guide. There is no alternative. That may sound harsh but that is the crude fact.

To say that is *not* to say that Islam (or Hinduism, or Buddhism) does not teach many valuable ideas. It is *not* to suggest that it is not worthy of respect. But it *is* to say that **if Jesus was uniquely God in human form then no religion can as truly reveal God as Jesus did.**

---

*But just how much can you rely on the Bible? In what sense, if any, is it true? This book is written on the assumption that it *is* a reliable record. If you are unsure about this then there are many books which argue the case for accepting the Bible's authority. You don't have to be an extreme Fundamentalist to find the Bible trustworthy.

Of course if Jesus was wrong, if he was only a man, if he didn't rise, then the field is wide open. You pays your money and you takes your choice.

But remember. Only one man has ever seriously claimed to be the very voice of God. And just suppose that he was right! That puts a very different complexion on things.

GOLD DUST

If he was right, then every word he spoke is gold dust. Every syllable he uttered, the one pure drop of water in a polluted stream of human babble down the centuries. If he was right, then those words are more important than anything all the world's greatest men have ever said.

If he was right then my whole destiny hinges on him. Remember that dog on the HMV records? He recognized his master's voice. Whose voice do you recognize?

Do you think you're what they say you are?

TIM Rice, who wrote the lyrics for *Jesus Christ Superstar*, posed that vital question. He also made it clear that his own answer was that Jesus of Nazareth is *not* God. Even so, the question intrigued him and a whole generation. Who was, or is, that Man?

Let's start by clearing a bit of the debris away. It does not matter one bit what he looked like, and it's probably no accident that we haven't got a portrait of him. Did he have a beard (that's what most people assume because lots of artists painted him that way) and did he have flashing eyes, a fine physique, long permed hair and so on? It doesn't matter in the slightest. Actually some of the earliest pictures didn't give him a beard or long hair—they showed him looking like a Roman with a pudding-basin cut and clean-shaven. It still doesn't matter. Forget it.

WHO ARE YOU?

Tim Rice was absolutely right. He doesn't ask,

'What did you look like?' He asks, 'Who are you?' That's the most important single question in the history of the human race!

Why? Answer: because if he was (and is) what he and his closest followers claimed, then we are dealing with the most important event in history. We are dealing with God all mixed up with man. Not just Someone beyond (who might not be there). Not just Someone inside me (who might be no more than a feeling). We are dealing with the Real Thing. And that is fantastic.

First of all, let's be clear that **a man called Jesus from the town of Nazareth really did live on this planet nearly two thousand years ago**. There's no reasonable doubt about that. It's also clear that **he must have been a very remarkable man or his influence wouldn't have lasted as it has**. Thirdly, it is undoubtedly true that **he was executed by the Romans in Jerusalem**. And, lastly, there is no doubt that **he founded a new organization, whose first members were a mixture of fairly ordinary Jewish men and women and who claimed that he had risen from the dead on the Sunday after his execution and that they had seen him and talked to him**. Evidence for all this can be found from early writers who were *not* Christians.

GOOD NEWS

Almost at once his followers began to start spreading around what they called 'the gospel' (the word means 'good news') of what he had said and done. Despite his own very cautious use of titles which a good Jew would tend to reserve for God alone, he did not stop them calling him 'the Son of God' and even, on occasions, the actual word 'God'. No decent, honest, godfearing Jew would have been anything but appalled at being himself described as 'God'. It would have been the ultimate blasphemy. Yet Jesus does not seem to have objected.

Think what that means. That means that Jesus must have been a blasphemer, an evil man, content to mislead people. Or it could mean that he was a madman who actually believed he *was* God. Hospitals for the mentally disturbed often contain people who think they are Napoleon or Alexander the Great or even God.

But such patients don't usually leave people astounded by their spiritual power and super-natural gifts. We all recognize that they are disturbed, unbalanced people. Yet no one seems to have given serious consideration to the idea that Jesus was mad. No one felt sorry for the chap.

Or, again, suppose he was a crook. He would have had to be a peculiarly diabolical rogue to do the good that he did and teach the Sermon on the

Mount. Crooks, by and large, simply aren't like that. And anyway what crook walks knowingly into a police trap with every expectation that he will meet his death at the end of the road? Men just aren't like that.

MAD, BAD OR . . .

So he wasn't profane or insane. He wasn't bad or mad. Which only leaves the possibility that he actually was divine. God. Those are the only logical possibilities. Deny that he was mad or that he was bad and you're left with the fact that he must have been God.

Well, not quite. He might simply have been wrong. Well-meaning but mistaken. Yes, I see what you mean but then how could he have risen from the dead? **His followers were utterly defeated men and women on the night of his death. Forty-eight hours later they were flabbergasted. In ones and twos, then a dozen at a time, more and more saw him alive until even five hundred saw him at one go.** And there was no body in the tomb which could have been produced to scotch the rumour.

Now if he was mistaken, how did he rise? And if (as some imply) the disciples had pinched the corpse and hidden it, how could others have seen him? And if it was all hallucination, would the bent disciples who had hidden the body be prepared to die simply to uphold what they knew to be a lie? It takes more swallowing than the truth itself.

So, Christians believed, as they do today, that God had entered into human life in the very fullest sense. He had been born of a very ordinary peasant mother, yet she was 'possessed' by the Spirit of God who enabled her, as a virgin, to conceive a child with no human father.

STRANGE

The strange fact is that the Jewish people did *not* expect their Messiah to be born of a virgin mother. The only possible reference in the Old Testament (Isaiah 7.14) means simply 'a young woman of marriageable age'. Despite this, Luke (writing for Greeks) and Matthew (writing for Jews) both begin their gospel accounts with absolutely explicit statements of Mary's physical virginity. Since the Jews didn't expect it and the Greeks didn't need it, why did the Christians, then and ever since, regard it as crucial—a matter to be included in the Creeds? It could only make belief harder, not easier. So why? The only likely answer is that they did so because they were convinced that it was true, however improbable it might seem.

Hard to believe? Yes, but then how much harder to believe that God could become man; that the infinite could become finite; that the

33

Lord of Glory could become a baby. I personally don't find the mechanics of a virgin conception or a resurrection are difficult to accept once you have grasped the incredible idea that God could actually become a real, flesh and blood man.

Where have we got to? **That Jesus the man of Nazareth was no less than the Creator of the Universe, the very Word of God in human form, born to a virgin mother. That he grew up and lived and taught and acted in such a way that those who knew him best** (and those nearest you usually know the worst about you) **believed him to be morally perfect and eventually came to describe him as God.** Remember, they were Jews and that admission of his 'God-ness' was the most blasphemously awful idea that could ever have entered a Jew's mind. Yet they couldn't and didn't shrink from it.

TITLES

They mentioned and gave him titles (or heard him use them of himself) which claimed that he was the source of all life, the only true way, the antidote to death. Fearful titles they were—only suitable to be used of God. Yet he used them and his life demonstrated that they were true because he could heal the sick and raise the dead and provide food and drink from nowhere and still storms and walk on the sea, and he so obviously wasn't a nutter!

It sounds like trick photography to us. It must have been absolutely terrifying to them. Yet they believed him. In awe and fear they believed him because his love and burning holiness were plain for all to see.

He knew who he was all right. Never once did they hint that he had any doubt. He was the unique Son of God. Everything that God was, he was. Everything that was made, he made.

'Who are you, Jesus Christ?' sings the *Superstar* chorus. To Christians, the answer to that is clear enough. He knew all right.

The King
of
Hearts

WHEN Jesus was first launched on an unsuspecting world, he began to talk about a kingdom. To most of us in the late twentieth century, kingdoms have little meaning, unless we happen to live in one of the fairly small number of states which are still ruled by kings or queens. Even then, the modern kingdom with its democratic government is a very different idea from that which Jesus was on about.

Kingdoms in his day were ruled by Kings. Real Kings (in the old sense) with unlimited power and authority. To most of us the idea isn't particularly appealing, because history shows us that most Kings of that kind were little better than bully-boys in crowns. You know the kind of thing. 'Do what I say or I'll chop your head off.' Or else they were pleasure-loving drifters who squandered everyone's money on fantastic palaces while the poor starved. Kings, by and large, weren't keen on letting other people in on the act—they liked being at the centre of the stage and expected everyone to say, 'Darling, you were marvellous' or whatever it is that flatterers say to kings. The result is that kings these days are a vanishing species. Perhaps someone ought to put a conservation order on those who are left before the species becomes extinct.

But just suppose a king were to be a just and perfect ruler. Life might be a lot easier than it is these days with everyone squabbling with everyone else—workers against bosses, blacks against whites, leftists against rightists. A kingdom could be quite something if it were to be a perfect society.

PERFECT

So Jesus talked about a perfect kingdom. He got the idea from the Old Testament where a number of the Jewish prophets had foretold a future time when God would appoint a 'Messiah' to rule. His kingdom, said the prophets, would be just and peaceful. It would embrace the whole world and it would last for ever. That was their dream—the same dream that Martin Luther King was to have in our century—and all good Jews looked forward to it—and many of them still do today.

But Jesus didn't look forward to it. **He began by telling people that it had already arrived. A new order had begun and 'the kingdom of heaven is here'.**

Now naturally any thoughtful Jew wasn't going to take much notice of *that* kind of talk.

37

'Give us some evidence,' they said. 'That'll soon sort him out,' they thought.

What shook them was that the Old Testament had given some fairly clear ideas about what sort of things the coming 'Messiah' would do. **He would give sight to the blind, he would enable the lame to walk, he would purify the leper, the deaf would hear—even the dead would be brought back to life**. 'That'll sort out this Jesus fellow,' thought some of the Jews. 'Let him have a go at that, for a start.'

Even today people still find it hard to believe that such miracles could have happened, but quite obviously no one who actually saw Jesus healing people could easily write off the evidence of his own eyes. It actually happened. Jesus was doing all the things a Messiah was supposed to do.

WE WANT A KING!

Except of course that he didn't do it the way they were all expecting. They had their eyes skinned, looking for a king with a crown and swords and trumpets and chariots and what have you. 'Give us a King in a gold-plated Rolls Royce, a star-studded Cadillac,' they pleaded. But Jesus wasn't having any.

'Listen,' he said, 'the kingdom of heaven is like . . . ' and then he told them stories (what we call 'parables') which showed clearly enough that

38

the kingdom was an inward thing to do with a man's heart. This King conquers men's hearts and rules there. And he conquers with the truth of his gospel which frees men from all the other slaveries of pride and greed and lust and selfishness.

Next time you look at the famous 'Sermon on the Mount' (Matthew 5–7), you'll see that it begins with the ideals of the kingdom. **'Happiness,' says Jesus, 'comes to those who acknowledge their own poverty, those who want to see right come out on top, those whose hearts are pure.'** The whole of that sermon is about the Kingdom and how these ideals relate to the Old Testament, to the various religious practices like prayer and fasting and almsgiving, to the ordinary problems of everyday life—greed, anxiety, bitchiness and the need to tell good from bad. **Everyone can see at a glance what a tremendous sermon it is, but not everyone sees that it is a kind of Magna Charta—the great charter of freedom for the just Kingdom**.

But there was a shock still to come to those who followed Jesus in those days. They were amazed by his power and swept along by his personality but they couldn't see that the crunch was coming. But Jesus could. When Peter, the very first of his followers, actually came out into the open and declared, 'You are the Messiah,' Jesus told him that he had to suffer and die. 'God forbid,' said Peter. 'That's not what Messiahs are here for.' But he was wrong. Jesus did wear a crown all right—but it was made of vicious spiked thorns. Jesus did carry an orb and sceptre all right—but it was a reed. He got his royal purple robe—and then Roman soldiers jeered at him, spat in his eye and fell on their knees in mock homage, splitting their sides with obscene laughter. They even scrawled 'King of the Jews' on a bit of wood and nailed it up over his head on the cross.

CROWNED

So Jesus got his crown all right. But he worked for it. He sweated and bled and died for it. None of which would have done him any good if he hadn't been king by divine right. But because he didn't need men to tell him he was king he shattered that tomb—and everyone else—and lives, and lives, and lives. In the great vision of the apostle John (which we call the Book of Revelation) he was, and is, 'in the middle of the throne' in heaven. So maybe that is just picture language—or maybe it's not—it doesn't matter. What does matter is that a King came, earned his kingdom and has claimed it.

Next time round, so he said, there'll be no mangers and cowsheds. Next time there'll be trumpets and the King will be requiring the account books to be opened. Next time round there'll be an almighty reckoning to be sorted out. First, justice. Then, peace.

And where will we stand when they come to sort out the justice bit? Will we still be around when they get to the peace bit or will the judge have sent us down first? Because you can only have perfect kingdoms if the imperfect have first been kicked out. So let's hope you're perfect.

You aren't? Read on, there may still be time.

It was on a Friday morning

BLOOD and flies and humiliation and pain, God,
the pain never stops. Every muscle taut as a bow-
string, shattered hands, mangled feet, a back
shredded by whips into quivering red meat. More
dead than alive before being nailed on to the
wooden gibbet and now one throbbing,
excruciating, ceaseless torment. And they call it
crucifixion. The Assyrians invented it but their
method was too quick. They merely impaled you
on a sharpened stake, up the anus, through the
body, and out through the mouth. You didn't last
long. So the Romans perfected it, dragged it out
longer, refined it, in order to let you have a little
time to meditate upon your crimes. By the second
or third day, four-fifths crazed as the crows peck
your eyes out, maybe (or so the Romans calculated) you'll act as a fairly effective deterrent to
other would-be opponents of the regime.

OBSCENE

No wonder the sight was obscene. No wonder the
Romans themselves shrank from such enormity

and only inflicted it upon slaves and subject peoples. However guilty, no Roman citizen must ever meet such a fate. So ran the law. For Romans, the sword or the axe. A quick, clean death. But for rebellious tribesmen and for disobedient slaves—well, they were not *real* men anyway, little better than wild animals, so a harsh lesson, a good flogging (some died at that stage), and nail them up by the side of the road outside the town.

But then even crucifixion didn't seem to stop those Jews. Quinctilius Varus had put down a revolt in Jerusalem back in 4 BC. It never stood a chance but that didn't move Varus's heart one bit. 'Nail them up,' he ordered, and his legionaries crucified the best part of two thousand young Jews along the roadsides. They chopped down acres of woodland to do it, but they did it all right. The Romans always were an efficient lot. Seventy years later Titus repeated the lesson and ran out of trees for crosses.

MORE PAIN

All those thousands of crucifixions, agonized men, weeping women and yet just one has come down through history. Jesus, the field-preacher from Nazareth. So why was his crucifixion any different from all the rest? Did he suffer more? Was the pain worse? Haven't others been tortured more cruelly and for far longer? So why pick on his crucifixion and blow the story up as if he was the only one to know what it felt like?

That's a good question. It's true that the Christian Church—especially the Roman Catholic Church—has tended to lay great stress on the physical sufferings of Jesus. Millions of crucifixes, large and small, have kept the figure of a dying Christ before people's eyes. Hundreds of paintings have depicted the gruesome pallor and the pain-wracked body. It's hardly surprising that for many people this crucifixion is the only one they've ever heard about.

But the question remains. Why stress this one crucifixion when there were so many others?

There's a very simple answer to that. This crucifixion was different. Different, not in the sense that there was more pain or less pain, but, nevertheless, different in that something extra, and at a totally new level, was taking place.

LIFE AND DEATH

The gospel accounts—Matthew, Mark, Luke and John—set aside a huge proportion of their time and space to the description of the last hours of the life of Jesus. Most biographies are all about someone's life and only a page or so about their death. The gospels say a lot about Christ's life but nearly a third of their space is about his death.

Even stranger, they hardly do more than

mention the actual fact of his bodily suffering. No stress whatever on the torture—much, much less than I've done in this chapter. Now why is that? There's little doubt that he *did* suffer in the way I've described, yet the Gospels say almost nothing about it. So obviously the real meaning of the Crucifixion isn't just a matter of physical pain. What's the secret?

The three accounts of the Gospel by Matthew, Mark and Luke tell the story of Jesus in, broadly speaking, very much the same way. They make it plain that he knew he was going to die. He never flinches from going onwards to the capital city, Jerusalem, even though he often warned his followers that it would mean his death.

So he spoke of his death. But only twice did he ever tell them why it was necessary for him to have to die. **Once, on the road near Jericho, Jesus spoke of his coming death as 'a ransom'. The second time, only hours before the crucifixion, he said that his blood was to be 'poured out for the forgiveness of sins'.**

RANSOM

There have been enough kidnappings and hijackings in recent years for everyone to know what a 'ransom' is. A ransom is the price paid to save another person's life. So, according to Jesus, the price to be paid for the forgiveness of mankind's sins was nothing less than the pouring out of his own life blood on the Cross. He knew, in other words, that his death was to have far greater meaning than simply the suffering of physical pain. He was to be involved in a unique act of sacrifice in order to deal once and for all time with the fact of human self-centredness, pride, and disobedience—the cancer at the heart of man's motives, attitudes and actions which we call sin.

The Bible says with utter simplicity 'he bore our sins'. You remember how he cried out, 'My God, my God, why have you abandoned me?' Well, that must have been a desolate moment for him. He had always spoken of God as his 'Daddy' (yes, he actually did use the child's loving, trusting word) and suddenly something fearful had wrenched them apart. That something was your sin and mine, because he who was sinless was, as Paul put it starkly, 'made *to be sin*'.

It's hard for the horror to break in on us. We simply don't know what it feels like to be perfect and then to have to carry all the world's filth round on our shoulders. We're too used to the filth, the sin and the guilt to be able to feel what he felt.

Try thinking of it this way. If I were to see a man drown in a cesspool full of human sewage, I should probably be sick and shocked at the utter filthy horror of the spectacle. That's what happened to Jesus. The only difference is that the

46

sewage which drowned him was moral not material. It was the cesspool of human sin which drowned him and he swallowed it to the very end.

NAUSEA

Someone once asked me not to be so repulsive as ever to use that illustration again. But I refused. Of course it nauseates us, makes us want to vomit. Yet how strange that we can look at the crucifixion quite unmoved! If ever anything should shatter our complacency that should. 'He bore our sins.' Does that disgust you? My God, it ought to!

But disgust is not enough. It ought to make me realize that *my* sin put him there. That he was dying for me. That I am the guilty sinner and he the innocent victim who chose to hang there on my behalf. It ought to put me on my knees crying 'Sorry' and 'Thank you' with the same breath. It ought to smash my self-righteousness once and for all. That's what Bloody Friday was all about.

But those who stood watching knew nothing of this. They thought it was the end of Jesus. So they put him into a rock tomb, sealed it, put a guard on it, rubbed their hands with satisfaction and went home to supper.

Night fell and blotted out the hopes of his followers. Who could possibly have guessed that God had an ace up his sleeve?

Missing: believed alive

SUNDAY by Sunday, millions of Christians the world over say in chorus these extraordinary words: **'the third day he rose again from the dead'**.

The significance of that event has never been so briefly or so starkly presented as it was by Michael Ramsey on a David Frost television interview. Ramsey, who was Archbishop of Canterbury at the time, put it in four words, 'No resurrection, no Christianity'.

Clearly then there can be no more important historical fact than this in all history. If Jesus did not die and rise again, then the whole Christian thing is exploded as a lie.

DID HE DIE?

So there are two questions to answer: is it certain that he really did die and is it certain that he actually returned from the dead? Some supposedly clever men have suggested that Jesus was not really dead at all but fainted and later recovered in the cool of the rock tomb. Could that in fact be what happened?

No, it couldn't. And why can we be so sure? Four reasons. The earliest written account says that the crucifixion took place on the day before an important Jewish Sabbath and a second account makes it clear that it was important to the Jews that the body of Jesus (and those of the two criminals executed with him) should not be allowed to remain on public display as it would defile the Sabbath. Thus they asked for all three to be finished off by the soldiers before dusk. Pilate the governor authorized this and the other two were killed. The account goes on to record that when the soldiers reached Jesus 'they found that he was already dead'. **First reason** then: the soldiers knew he was dead (and soldiers aren't exactly inexperienced at knowing death when they see it).

CHECK IT OUT

On to reason number two. One of Jesus' friends was a rich man called Joseph of Arimathea. He plucked up his courage, went to Pilate and asked for the body. Naturally Pilate checked first with the military authorities (the account records this) and only when the officer in charge of the execution squad had certified that Jesus was dead was Joseph authorized to remove it. **Reason two**: Pilate, the Roman governor, knew that Jesus was dead — he checked it to make sure.

Reason three: next morning the Jewish authorities called on Pilate and referred to a prophecy which Jesus had made 'while he was still alive'. So the account runs. The wording cannot but mean that they now believed him to be both dead and buried. So reason three is that the Jewish authorities were satisfied that he was dead.

The **final reason** is that the Christians undoubtedly believed that he was dead. His beloved young friend John says that he actually saw the evidence of the ruptured heart from which Jesus had died and he goes on to say that his evidence was that of an eyewitness and 'is to be trusted'. Moreover the women who went to the tomb with their spices and perfumes at the ready clearly knew him to be dead.

It is conceivable that the women might have only *thought* he was dead. What is inconceivable is that the execution squad, the Roman authorities, the Jewish authorities and the one Christian who got close enough actually to see evidence of death were all fooled.

DID HE RISE?

So that brings us to question two: did he really rise? We've seen that any theory which suggests that since he wasn't dead he merely came to and escaped falls down because, first, he was pronounced officially dead and, in any case, he was tightly wrapped in bandages, weighed down with well over half a hundredweight of spices, sealed off by a huge stone over the tomb exit and desperately crippled in hands, feet and back.

But what other facts emerge? One thing is certain. The tomb was empty. No one disputes that except those who say that the authorities, the guards and the Christians mixed the tomb up with another one (and it wouldn't have been difficult for the authorities to check up on other tombs in the vicinity and triumphantly produce the body, would it?).

So the tomb was empty. But where was the body? The only people who could have had it were either the authorities or Jesus' friends. If it was the authorities then they had only to produce it. Instead they announced that the Christians had pinched it and were now claiming a resurrection.

There is no reason to doubt that the Christians were utterly broken by the death of Jesus. All the accounts agree about that. Yet by Sunday night they were stunned at the news—some of them had *seen* Jesus alive and well, and living in Jerusalem! And the whole lot lived and died (many by violent means) convinced that it was true. Yet, if they had actually stolen the body, no one ever leaked the truth and all were totally changed men prepared to die themselves. It is just not credible. Human beings do not and never have behaved like that.

WRAPPED UP

And then there were those bandages. You remember how they had wrapped Jesus in linen strips? Yet when Peter entered the tomb the linen bandages were still there undisturbed. So how do you account for that? It would seem that somehow the body was, in some strange way, able to pass right through the tight wrappings and leave them behind undisturbed. Now if he had simply revived and found himself wrapped tightly in bandages he would presumably have had a great job extricating himself and the bandages would have been left all over the place. If, on the other hand, his body was stolen it is hardly likely that the thieves would have unwrapped the corpse—they would almost certainly have picked up the encased body and gone.

All of which added together makes quite a case for the fact of the resurrection. An empty tomb, a whole range of witnesses (a dozen or more different incidents involving well over five hundred people, according to the Bible) and the silent linen wrappings, all combine to make a case which two thousand years of ingenious and sceptical unbelief has never looked like cracking. And just to clinch it, even Josephus, a non-Christian Jew writing in the later years of the first century, refers to the fact that Jesus 'appeared to them alive again on the third day as the divine prophets had foretold'. Those words are quite extraordinary, for Josephus was a pro-Roman Jewish collaborator who had nothing to gain by mentioning Jesus—yet he did so. He may or may not have believed it but he didn't hesitate to say that that was what the Christians believed.

DEAD TWICE?

So there, in a nutshell, is the case for the resurrection. But there's one last thing to add. Many people seem to be able to say 'on the third day he rose again' and yet in their hearts they then add 'and presumably at some later date died again'. To them, Jesus is essentially a figure of the long dead past. But that's not what Christians believe. **If Jesus rose that means he's alive today, that he has never died a second time, that he is our contemporary.**

Which is why the Bible accounts go on to speak of his having 'ascended into heaven'. Now whatever or wherever heaven may be, the point is that he has returned to the highest place of all, the very presence of God.

That's how it was that Jesus, God-made-man, played the power game, looked beaten, yet won a clinching victory for all time (and eternity, too) and returned to prove that he was the Lord of all creation.

And, going, he has not left us alone.

Power
to all
our friends

I ONCE came across a young woman who wanted very much to become a Christian but was worried at the thought of having, all alone, to try to live a good life. Lots of people make that same mistake—they think that Christians are left to sink or swim. There wouldn't be many Christians about if that was the case.

Jesus knew perfectly well that life is a tough business. He also knew that his followers would feel lost after his ascension. 'Don't be distressed,' he said. **'I will not leave you to face life all alone. The Father will give you another Helper to be with you for ever.' And just so that they would know exactly what he meant, Jesus called the Helper 'the Spirit of truth' or 'the Holy Spirit'.**

ENERGY

Now a good Jew, in those days, would certainly recognize the title 'the Spirit'. The Hebrew word actually meant 'wind' or 'breath' and a Jew knew that the Spirit was simply a vivid way of describing the living energy of God which could come upon a man and give him special powers—courage, wisdom, creative artistry and, perhaps especially, the gift of prophecy. Many times the Old Testament speaks of 'the Spirit of the Lord' that came upon this or that man.

There was nothing new then in Jesus' promise of the Spirit—or was there? Yes, there was—one quite new and special fact. To the Jews, the Spirit was no more than God's power. Jesus introduced the Spirit as 'him'—a personal, living power—and not just an 'it'. When Jesus left his friends and returned to his Father in his risen, glorified body he promised that *he* would come to them, no longer bound by a physical body but just as personal as ever. To those who continued to love him, Jesus added that he and his Father would 'come to him and make our home with him'. How was such a thing possible? Only through the living presence of the Holy Spirit—unseen, yet experienced at all times by the follower of Christ.

EXPERIENCE

Experienced? Yes, indeed, though not always recognized. So what does that mean for me? Let's take it stage by stage.

In the first few lines of the Bible we are introduced to the Spirit (or 'wind') of God, active in the very work of creation. It can fairly be said that Christians understand *all* creativity as springing from the very nature of the Spirit so that, in one sense, God works in everything and without his ceaseless activity nothing would exist at all. He is, as the theologians would say, both the source and the agent of all power.

So my very life depends for its being on him. He is the life-giver to all and we all experience what it means to be alive. Jesus, however, added a completely new dimension when he said that men needed not only to be *born* and thus to be, humanly speaking, given life but that man needed to be *re-born* and given a new kind of life and that this was a unique work of the Spirit. It must have shaken Nicodemus, a very religious Jew, to be told by Jesus (John's Gospel, chapter 3) that even he, in effect, needed to be re-born by the Spirit. How would you react if you were a famous religious leader—let's say you were a bishop—and were unexpectedly told that you needed to go back and start all over again? Nobody likes to be told such a thing. Yet that's what Jesus says to all of us, **'You need to be born all over again'**.

So the Spirit not only gives physical life to our bodies. He also gives us spiritual life, or you might say, *real* life. Indeed, the apostle Paul says quite bluntly that if you don't posses the Spirit then you aren't a Christian at all. All your praying, church-going, being decent, and so on—all in vain, says Paul, if the Spirit isn't in control of you!

THE PRICE

Now that's a blow to our pride because it strikes at the very root of the 'natural' human desire to be self-dependent. But that's the price we have to pay. We call it 'natural' to be self-dependent. God calls it natural for his creatures to acknowledge their utter dependence on him. His power is only available to those who acknowledge the limitations of their own power and, indeed, go further and recognize that they have no power of their own—it all comes from God and is all dependent on him.

And that's the point at which I come alive. When I come to see that I'm a disobedient, rebellious, sinful and proud little creature and such a realization breaks me up, then God's Spirit points out that Christ died for just such people and as I turn thankfully to him the new life flows through me. I've been reborn!

In recent years the mass media have taken to describing certain Christians as 'born again'. As usual they've got it wrong! According to the New Testament every genuine Christian has been 'born again'. There really is no such animal as a 'once born' Christian.

It may not be plain sailing from that new birth on (it isn't) but at least God's wind is in my sails and I'm heading for the right port. From now on I genuinely want God's wind—his Spirit—to fill my sails. 'Be filled with the Spirit', urged Paul. So I too want to catch the wind and ride it and **God promises that wind to me. It's his power for living. I'm not on my own any more**.

LOTS OF FRUIT

Let's change the picture from sea to land. The Bible tells me that the Spirit ensures that I am fruitful. Like a tree full of vigour I shall bear fruit in my character. Nine varieties are mentioned. The shopping list reads like this: **love, joy, peace, patience, kindness, goodness, fidelity, gentleness and self-control. That's what people are actually meant to be like**. The world would solve its problems tomorrow if they were! But then the world knows better than God's Spirit—and pays the price every day.

There's one more satisfying thing about the Spirit's work in our lives. Like any well-brought up guest he brings presents. Some of the presents are fairly everyday things (rather as we might give tea-towels and so on). Gifts like that of being good at organizing things or patching things up when others get hurt. Sometimes the gifts are more exciting and decorative. Just as you might give someone a beautiful glass ornament, an eye-catching picture or a tape of a famous piece of music, so too God's Spirit can pass on the gift of inspiring speech or great wisdom or even the ability to perform miracles or to be carried away in ecstatic words. All the gifts—penny plain or two-pence coloured—are there to strengthen and build up the family of Christians. They aren't meant to make us proud or jealous or depressed—we all get something from the Spirit—but rather to make us useful to God and our fellow men.

BAD FEELING

Frankly, it's a sad fact that in recent years there's been a lot of bad feeling created concerning the work of God's Spirit. Some say he works this way, others that. People get overexcited and blame other Christians. Books get written and speeches made many of which are terribly one-sided.

Yet despite all of this, God's Spirit is at work. Sometimes quietly, privately, and in very ordinary ways; sometimes in great sweeping acts of widescale significance. At the heart of both there is all the power of God made available to men. Power—that's the key word. As the song says—'Baby, power to you and me'.

Three
into one
won't go!

BELIEVING in one God as maker and preserver of
the universe makes reasonable sense to over half
of the world's population and according to most of
the opinion polls they claim to believe in such a
God. Probably about a quarter claim to believe
that Jesus is himself God in human form. Fewer
still know what to make of the Holy Spirit. But
these three are child's play compared to understanding and believing in the Trinity—one God
and yet three persons. The only thing to do with
that doctrine is to stamp it 'too difficult' and
return it to the makers as not wanted.

EQUATION

Which is what the Jehovah's Witnesses do. They
try to be clever by reducing it all to arithmetic.
Their sum looks something like this:

$$1 + 1 + 1 = 3$$

That, they say, proves that you can't have
'three persons and one God'. The only alter-

natives, they say, are to have three persons who are three Gods (like the Mormons) or one God and two other rather special characters (who don't rate quite in the God class). The latter is roughly the Jehovah's Witness way of trying to resolve it all.

A BETTER ONE

Despite all that, Christians, frankly, aren't impressed. Playing with arithmetic about such a matter is hardly the most satisfactory way of trying to get to grips with it at first sight and any fool knows that *adding* is not the only way of arranging numbers. Why not do the sum this way?

Which nevertheless proves nothing on its own about the Trinity. Funnily enough, as we shall see, arithmetic *does* enter into it (even in the Bible), but that isn't the place to start. So we'll start with the Jewish belief in One God.

Probably the most fundamental belief of the Jews (and therefore of the whole Bible) is the belief that there is one God and one God only. Nowhere could a Jew (or a Christian, for that matter) seriously consider that there might be three Gods. There must be an ultimate unity underlying everything and the idea of more than one God would totally destroy that.

Remember, then, that the earliest Christians were all Jewish men and women who neither did, nor ever could have denied the unique one-ness of God. Yet they heard Jesus claim, and they came to accept his claim, that he was 'one with the Father'. He told them that 'he who has seen me has seen the Father'; that 'I am in the Father and the Father in me', and they heard him pray to that same Father (God) and say that he and his Father were one. Three times in the prayer he repeated it. To a good Jew that was either blasphemy of the most fearful kind, or else something completely new was happening. So, almost reluctantly, they came to see that the person they called Jesus, while clearly a real man, was also something far greater. They were to write of him as having been 'with God from the beginning of all things', as having himself 'made the worlds' and, indeed, that he actually 'was God'. Three times they called him the 'image' of God (and Jews totally forbid images) and spoke of him as being of the very 'substance' of God. God's fullest reality lived within him bodily.

THREE PERSONS

And then there was the Spirit. According to Jesus, the Spirit came from within the very character of God and Jesus called the Spirit not 'it', but 'he'. A number of places in the New Testament ascribe to the Spirit what the Old Testament ascribes to God. Five times Father, Son and Spirit are joined together in a way that leaves little doubt that the early Christians had learnt to recognize the 'God-quality' of all three, all of whom were in some way personal and were both three and yet one. Perhaps the best statement comes from Paul who, calling on Christians to be *united*, made his point by saying that there was one Spirit, one Lord and one Father God.

But let's go back to the arithmetic. You will have no difficulty in recognizing this mathematical shape:

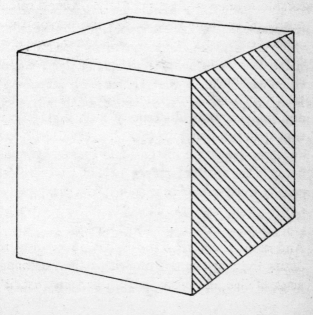

It is of course, a cube. Its length, breadth, and height are all equal. Without those three dimensions it could have no real existence (since a square or a single line must have some depth or else they have no reality except as mathematical ideas). So a cube is three-dimensional. Yet the actual content of length, breadth and height are all the same. But length is not breadth and neither is to be confused with height. So a cube is both three and one at the same time. What is more, you cannot remove any one dimension without destroying all three since all three hang together to make up the one unity.

Well, so what? That's mere arithmetic. Yes, but the surprising thing is that when the Bible wants to describe the very presence of God, it is the cube which is the figure which is given by God himself. In the Old Testament, that part of the Temple which was the most sacred place of all—the place in which God's very glory was to be found—was built as a perfect cube. It was a symbol, *the* symbol, of the reality of God.

TO COME?

Turn to the end of the New Testament and you find John's vision of the heavenly city of God. And what shape is it to be? Right first time. The city—God's very presence in symbolic form—is a perfect cube and we are told that it shines 'with the glory of God' (the very word which had been used to describe the presence of God in the Temple's holiest place).

So arithmetic isn't after all irrelevant. But only the most unimaginative man or woman would think that God actually *looks* like a cube. The Trinity is, after all, the most mysterious of all doctrines and no man can ever grasp the full reality of its meaning. Many have tried and the most detailed formula is to be found in the so-called 'Athanasian Creed' in the Church of England's Book of Common Prayer.

Most ordinary Christians probably find themselves grateful to the person who once said: 'If the reality of God were small enough to be grasped, it would not be great enough to be adored.'

That gets to the heart of the matter.

The God squad

WHEN Peter got all hot and bothered about the terrible idea of the Messiah having to suffer and die, he was only reacting in a perfectly natural way. Natural for a Jew of his day, but also natural for a 'normal' human being in any age. To him—and there are many like him today—winning was what matters. Messiah must be seen to have come out on *top*, he must be on show saluting at victory parades, he must be the successful executive smiling behind his desk.

But Peter was forgetting something. Jewish history up to his time (it's in the Old Testament) had been marked by three parallel strands, three great complementary ideas.

JUSTICE

First there was the kingly idea and the hope of a Messiah. That was certainly a success-oriented idea concerned with ruling and justice. But the key was justice—not success.

Secondly there was the priestly idea—the need for a means of removing sin by sacrifice through the prayers and actions of a priesthood.

Lastly there was the task of the prophet. He had to proclaim the truth fearlessly even if it meant unjust treatment and terrible suffering in return. Isaiah (one of them) spoke movingly of a 'Suffering Servant'.

Peter, then, had to learn to see Christ's mission as related to all three and the fulfilment of all three. How well he learnt that lesson can be seen in his first letter (1 Peter) **contained in the New Testament. There he speaks of God having called into being a People (not just individuals) who are to be royal, priestly and prophetic. They are to offer 'spiritual sacrifices', they are to proclaim Christ's triumph and—and this bit is repeated over and over again—they must suffer faithfully as Christ himself did.** Gone is the easy success and the short-term popularity. And in its place the certainty of a mission, which, despite the desperate battering inevitably launched upon it by the powers of evil, will be ultimately vindicated and seen to be triumphant at the glorious return of Christ, the Messiah, at the end of the age.

MISSION

That, in a nutshell, is the mission of the God-squad, the task of the church which Jesus founded.

Down the ages that mission has often been

obscured and corrupted but always there have been those who stayed faithful to God's calling. But the sad result of the distortions of history is that many people—perhaps the majority of those in the Western nations—now have such a confused notion of what the church is meant to be that they dismiss it as an irrelevance. Westerners today use the word when they mean 'the clergy' ('he's gone into the church'); the institution ('why doesn't the church say something'); the building ('they were married in church') and so on.

Jesus himself said that he had come to 'build' his church on a rock, and that the rock—the foundation—was to be a confession of faith in himself as God's chosen Messiah. If you can't declare your faith in him, then you can't be part of his church, and the foundation rock has become instead a stumbling-stone over which you can trip and fall.

NOT A PLACE

The very word 'church' is interesting. It comes from a Greek word *ecclesia* and means a group of people who have been called out. What is quite certain is that it *never* meant 'building' or 'institution' or 'clergy'. The church is people—believing, Christian people—and the Bible uses a number of pictures to describe their relationship.

Christians see themselves as brothers and sisters, all children of the same Father, by whose Spirit they have been reborn into his Family.

Elsewhere it speaks of Christians as living stones, all joined together to make a living Temple. Each interlocked stone supports and holds the others in place and only thus can the living Temple be a strong building.

Perhaps the most striking picture used is that of the Body. Christ is the head and his followers are all limbs and organs. Each has a different job to do but each needs the others if the body is not to be maimed and disabled.

Now these three pictures (and there are others) are very simple and everyone can grasp the idea. Christ has founded a new and living group and there is only one. Down through the ages there have been thousands of local offshoots all over the world but the church is still *one* body. Even though Christians have disagreed and divided up into different so-called denominations (Roman Catholics, Eastern Orthodox, Methodist, Lutheran, Brethren etc.), there is still only one church to which all faithful Christians belong.

WHICH ONE?

It happens that I belong to the Church of England. Some of my friends are members of churches holding very different views from mine. For example I greatly value the historical links which have kept the word 'Catholic' meaningful to members of the Anglican Communion (of which the Church of England is part). But I certainly don't use the word in the same way that a Roman Catholic would and I genuinely think he is wrong. So too some of my Baptist friends would be very uneasy about my understanding of the need for the different denominations to seek a real visible unity, that's to say to show some public signs of being *one* church. The Roman Catholic and the Baptist both think I'm mistaken. I confess on occasions that I feel the same way about them. Even in an ecumenical age when most Christians are cautious about making hurried judgements about those in other churches, it can still be hard to find common ground about the nature of the church and how Christ meant his church to function.

I believe that to be a true follower of Christ is to be a member of the true church which he founded. Yet that membership is meaningless unless I share in a local Christian fellowship. So I want to be part of **a church which seeks to be holy, catholic, apostolic and one. Those are the great words used in the early Christian Creeds and I cannot lightly ignore them**.

But what do they mean? To *be* one is surely more than just to *feel* one. So I must seek a church which is concerned with outward as well as 'spiritual' unity. To be apostolic is to have concern for the truths which the apostles taught so I shall not be at ease among those who deny such truths. To be catholic is to recognize the world-wide and timeless nature of the church of Christ (and also that there are limitations to truth i.e. that heresy does exist and such bodies are *outside* the church catholic). Finally, to be holy is to seek to be, as a group, made like Christ through his Spirit's power.

FAR SHORT

Still it has sadly to be admitted that Christ's prayer for his church (John's Gospel, chapter 17) is still a long way short of fulfilment. We aren't perfect yet, and although Christ's holy church will one day be perfected, all the local versions are a long way off being the 'unblemished virgin bride' which the Bible pictures. Which is, however, no excuse for opting out and starting your own show. People have tried that out time after time. It usually leads to more splits.

It's no accident that babies can't choose their own families—they're born into one. So we too when re-born by Christ's Spirit aren't meant to start up our own family but rather to share in his Family—first as newborn babes and then to full maturity. The God-squad, as Christ means it to be, is the most satisfying family of all, because through Christ's blood we're all blood relations.

I've got
you under
my skin

THE Church of Jesus Christ has been around a lot longer than I have, and because of all its divisions I could very well be forgiven for thinking that so long as I turn up at the local branch office every so often all will be well. I can't remember who it was who called such people 'Four-wheeler Christians' because the only times they put in an appearance, they turned up in a pram, a wedding-car or a hearse. In other words, when they were bred, wed, and dead!

NO MUSEUM

Now if you've got this far in this book you'll know that such an attitude simply isn't on. Jesus didn't die so that a new kind of religious museum might be opened in every town and village. He called for followers (the word means 'to take the same road') and he meant his followers to be committed whole-heartedly to him.

I once had a friend who was a football fan. He came from Britain's so-called 'Black Country' and he was an utterly dedicated supporter of Wolverhampton Wanderers. We used to meet every Monday morning and I could tell in a flash as he came through the door whether Wolves had won or lost on the previous Saturday.

Some time later I spent three years in Liverpool and every so often the two great rival clubs—Liverpool and Everton—would meet in a clash of the giants. Since the city was football-crazy and divided roughly half and half in support, you could be certain that roughly a quarter of a million people would be wild with triumph and another quarter million down in the dumps for at least a week after the match.

Those two examples show precisely what it means to be a follower. Jesus called for followers.

THAT THREE-LETTER WORD

And yet there's even more to it than that. A sports fan may be deeply committed to his team but such a relationship isn't the closest known to man. Pick up one of the popular newspapers and glance at it quickly. What's it all about? That's right. Sport and ... sex!

Why sex? Well, surely because it is through the total sense of oneness which is what sex, at its most meaningful, is all about, that men and women feel their humanity's fulfilment. The Bible always describes that by saying that a couple 'know' each other.

Isn't it fascinating to realize that the Bible also uses that same word 'know' to describe the utter sense of oneness which Christ shares with those who are really committed to him? 'Christ in you' is, says Paul, the tremendous, glorious and hopeful experience available to every Christian. **To 'know' Christ is to be assured of his presence within me and, even when I don't consciously 'feel' that presence, to be as certain as a human being can be that he *is* one with me and I with him**.

Yes, but how? How can you *start*? I remember a young man in his twenties asking me that very question. It's all well and good for you, he said. You've got going and it all makes sense. But how do I begin? What's more, he went on, I don't think I've got enough faith.

Let's take the last point first. Many people have said these words to me over the years. 'Not enough faith.' Three tragic words because they reveal a simple but terrible misunderstanding. To those who use them it all seems clear enough. Some people have faith. Some haven't. I haven't. Tough luck. Poor me.

TRY A VERB

The mistake is this. Faith is not a commodity like money which some have and some haven't. Faith is no more than a noun for the *act of believing*.

For many years I have stood in church buildings and married hundreds of young couples. They come in un-married. They go out

74

man and wife. At one point in the service they take each other's hand and say 'I will'. That's the key moment because that's the act of faith, the decisive second at which they say 'Yes'. That's what faith is.

Gamblers do it all the time. Out comes the money. 'Pink Pantaloons, on the nose, for the 3.15.' 'You're on,' says the bookmaker and, win or lose, you've exercised faith. You've committed yourself.

Nobody, repeat nobody, ever became a Christian in the real sense unless he was prepared to do that. For some people the process leading up to the moment of commitment may have been long drawn out and they slip over the line almost without knowing it. For others it is absolutely decisive and clearcut. The method is quite unimportant. The actual commitment is everything. You either do or you don't.

Human beings are, of course, changeable creatures and God knows that very well. That's why the bride has a ring and the gambler gets a ticket. It proves that the marriage (or the bet) is on. It's a token of reassurance. It wasn't all fantasy. I did marry him, etc. etc.

WATER, BREAD AND WINE

God gives just such tokens. One is called baptism. By using the symbol of water, man is assured that he *is* washed, that God *has*

cleansed him, that the Spirit *has* begun to work out that new life in him. Every time the Christian doubts whether it's all true, this God business (and lots of Christians *do* have such doubts), he recalls the water and the promise and is given an encouraging reminder of God's love and faithfulness. It's called a 'sacrament'. And because being 'born-again' can only happen once so, too, baptism only happens once. We have, said Paul, 'One Lord, one faith, one baptism'.

The second token, or sacrament, is also a reminder to us. This time we take bread and wine and it forms for us a solemn guarantee that Christ himself, his body and his blood, really is within us. Unlike baptism, this is repeated because it speaks to us of constant spiritual nourishment, of food which keeps us alive and healthy. What's more, it's a kind of foretaste of that heavenly party we were thinking about earlier. It's such a sad thing to see the mournful way in which many churches conduct their holy communion services. Surely we are meant to be taking part in a warm, friendly, happy party? In the Church of England we use words like *celebration, joy*, and *praise* but you would think you were at a funeral half the time. Other churches are much the same. What we could do with is a bit more of a party atmosphere. After all, Christ not only died but rose again and that's well worth celebrating.

ESSENTIAL?

Of course, people sometimes say, 'Are these sacraments really necessary?' To which they frequently add, 'Surely, if I believe, surely that's all that really matters? The answer to that is that Christ didn't see it that way or he wouldn't have been so definite. 'Go and baptize,' he said to his followers. 'Take and eat,' he told them. 'Drink this,' he added. Who has the right to call himself a follower if he refuses to obey such direct commands?

Perhaps this is a good point to ask yourself some straight questions. Have I said 'Yes' to Christ? Have I been baptized and thus marked as one of his followers? Do I eat and drink as he commanded? That's what faith is all about. It's being prepared to gamble everything on the one great fact that Jesus *is* the one true God who alone has the answer for mankind.

Do I *really* have to make my mind up about that?

Yes, you do.

May
your God
go
with you

BEING one of Christ's followers is no joke. While
it is true that God's new life is a gift and you can't
earn it but only receive it with gratitude; while it
is true that there is nothing more satisfying in
the whole world than to be 'walking' with him
day by day; while it is true that there is joy, and
laughter, and purpose and a sense of direction;
while all these things are true it can't be denied
that the Christian life is no bed of roses.

To become a follower of Christ is to experience,
as Paul put it, a 'new creation', or a 'conversion'
(which means to be turned round). But that's not
the end—that's just the beginning.

LIFE STYLE

So what about the everyday business of *being* a
Christian? What kind of life-style is involved?

The answer to that is simple enough. No one
exact blueprint is available. Russians,
Brazilians, Eskimos, Australians, Nigerians,

Americans— all have different customs and ways of life. Christians in Switzerland may vary considerably from Christians in Hong Kong in all manner of ways. In that sense there is no one life-style.

But there is one thing all have in common and that's that all, allowing for their cultural differences, are aiming to be like Jesus Christ. 'He,' said Peter, his great friend, 'left you an example.' Paul put it this way. He called us to grow to 'mature manhood . . . measured by the full stature of Christ'. **Jesus then is our example. We want to be like him and, by the Spirit's power, one day we shall be!**

But how is this to come about?

There are three ways in which the great change can take place. They are not alternatives, they are all linked into each other. They concern our motives, our character and our relationships.

MERIT

Take the question of motives first. People who believe in a god, any god, usually have as their chief motive the desire to be accepted by the god. They try to be good, to be religious, to be holy and hope that their god will eventually reward them. All their lives they live in hope of being good enough or in fear of not being good enough. Their deepest motive is to make themselves fit for their god's favour.

Christians totally reject that motive. Their motive is exactly the opposite. **Christians *know* that they aren't good enough to win God's favour. They know that Christ's death has for ever destroyed the need for such an idea. He died to make it possible for them to be cleansed and forgiven *as a gift* not as a reward**.

So the Christian's greatest motive is to say 'Thank you' to God for that incredible love. The whole of their lives is meant to be one big **'Thank you'**. The question therefore arises 'How can I best say "thank you"?'

Jesus told his followers to worship God, to share the fellowship of other Christians, to unite in prayer and communion, to learn about God by studying the Bible and accepting the wise teaching of more experienced Christians. Only in such a way can people grow to maturity as Christians. In that way their one desire to say 'Thank you' is helped to find expression because in such a way they'll get to know God better and their 'thank you' will affect every part of their lives.

VIRTUES

That brings us to the second way. When your motive is right, the results will begin to affect your character. Remember when we were thinking about the Spirit's work we saw that

Paul likened the result to 'fruit'? He mentioned nine virtues. Let's look at them again.

The first three—love, joy and peace—are concerned with *internal concord*. They are the fundamental habits of my heart towards God. I love him because of his love, I am full of joy because of the new life he gives and I am at peace, for my sin and guilt has been removed.

The next trio—patience, kindness, goodness—are related to *social contact* and are the expression of my feelings for my fellows. I am patient because I remember God's patience with me even when I was difficult and unappreciative. I am kind and good because only in that way can Christ's generosity be seen by others. They must see his kindness and goodness in me.

Finally, Paul mentioned fidelity, gentleness and self-control. These form the basis of my behaviour and constitute my *personal conduct*. Fidelity means to be reliable, to be trustworthy. Gentleness means to be tamed (rather like 'breaking-in' a horse) and self-control speaks for itself.

These characteristics are, says Paul, the result of the work of the Spirit. They are very much more than just the natural ability some people have to be nice and friendly and polite. And, notice, they aren't aimed at squashing the life and vitality out of people. Far from it. They're much more directed at channelling and creatively using our personalities in such a way that everyone benefits. What a contrast to those who think they can steamroller everyone in sight simply because they have the pushing characteristics of the bully.

A change of motive and a change of character. And as we've already begun to see, that involves, thirdly, a change in my relationships. As the Old Testament put it **I am now called 'to love God with all my heart, soul, mind and strength' and 'to love my neighbour as myself'.**

IF ONLY...

How many times do you hear politicians, schoolteachers, parents, even clergy, say that the world would be a better place 'if only' such and such a thing could happen? Usually they mean 'if only people would be nicer to each other' or something like that.

Where the Bible is realistic is that it says bluntly, 'They won't be.' Only by means of a change as basic as a 'new birth' can my motives be changed, my character transformed and my relationships revolutionized. To be a Christian is to let Christ control my friendships, my sex life, my politics, my leisure, my work, my attitudes to class and colour, my standards of honesty, justice and compassion—absolutely everything.

NO JOKE

No—being one of Christ's followers is no joke. And, thank God, he hasn't left us alone to get on with it. That would be unbearably difficult. But we are fortunate. In the local Christian church we find—whether it be large or small—a group of brothers and sisters equally dedicated to the service of a master whose service is 'perfect freedom'. In the Bible we hear the voice of God speaking plainly and with authority, which is why Christians make a point of reading it and following its teaching.* And in the quietness of our own times alone with God we draw added strength. 'You,' said Jesus, 'shall receive power.' He it is who gives us the presence and strength of the Holy Spirit to his followers.

No, we are not alone. Our God goes with us.

*Perhaps the simplest and most easily readable version is called the *Good News Bible*. It is on sale in most bookshops.

Keep right on to the end of the road

WHEN I was a boy, I remember hearing an old Scottish singer on the radio called Sir Harry Lauder. He used to sing a mixture of comic and sentimental songs and, being Scots, he made sure that most of them were about Scotland. It's a modest Celtic habit much imitated by his successors. As I remember them, most of his ballads were sung in the thickest of Glaswegian accents and usually ended up in tears of amusement or emotion. One of the former was called 'Will you stop yer tickling, Jock' (largely incoherent Clydeside giggling) while chief of the latter was a martial tearjerker called 'Keep right on to the end of the road'. Lauder composed this when he got the news of his son's death in the First World War.

THE WAY

The words form a good Christian motto, because Jesus undoubtedly talked a lot about roads—their width, their direction and their destination.

He often encouraged his followers to think of their lives as a kind of pilgrimage along a not very easy track. John Bunyan took the idea and turned it into one of the most famous books in the English language. He called it *Pilgrim's Progress*.

I expect you've heard of Judy Garland. She was the actress Liza Minnelli's mother, and she made her name by singing 'Somewhere over the rainbow' in the motion picture of the *Wizard of Oz* back in the late nineteen-thirties. In the film she played the part of Dorothy, the little orphan girl, who was caught up by a cyclone and whirled away to the far-off land of Oz. There, lost and longing to get back to her home, she was told to 'follow the yellow brick road' which would lead her to the City of Emeralds.

Today, the world is full of Dorothys who have lost their way and don't know how to find it. That's why this book came to be written as a kind of 'yellow brick road' for ordinary people or, to go back to our earlier picture, as an attempt to break the code which so many find baffling and mysterious.

So now as we're coming towards the end let's look at one more question. Where is it all leading? Where is the end of the road?

WHERE TO?

In the days when most English-speaking people

knew the Bible they knew perfectly well that it spoke about a beginning when things all began and an end when, after the return of Christ, there would be a Last Judgement and the ushering in of an eternal and just Kingdom where God would reign for ever.

Nowadays people, if they bother to think about it at all, seem to fall into three main categories. A decreasing number believe that a perfect world will ultimately come. Two terrible wars and a nuclear age have put paid to most of that kind of optimism. Rather more people sadly admit that they expect the world to destroy itself sooner or later. A large third group (one poll said over 60% of Britons) believe there will be a Day of Judgement but, quite illogically, assume that most people will be all right and that therefore (according to 25% of Britons) Hell is not a reality.

Strange, isn't it? More than twice as many people say they believe in Heaven as believe in Hell. Yet our world is full of evil, dishonesty, violence, greed and so on. Where are all these Heaven-dwellers going to be found? And what is going to happen to all the baddies if there is neither Judgement nor Hell?

PERFECT

The fact is, of course, that for most people the whole thing is no more than wishful thinking. But because we would all *like* to think that something nice is round the corner is no guarantee that any such thing exists. People who think like this are simply being shallow. Look at it this way. Heaven, if it is to have any attraction, needs to be perfect. Any God worth his salt must surely himself be perfect. So where are all the perfect people going to come from? Suppose we say that God will overlook their badness? That means that God is prepared to compromise with evil and thus become evil himself. That won't do. Couldn't he forgive them? But to forgive is not the same as to cleanse. They would still be evil, even if forgiven, so Heaven would still be full of evil people, all ready to go on being evil as before.

It just won't do. Evil must be dealt with, removed, got rid of. But what if people don't *want* to be made clean? Ought God to get them by the scruff of the neck? That would destroy human freewill and turn us all into puppets.

It all comes down to this. Christ came to deal with sin on the Cross, to offer forgiveness to those who wanted to be cleansed, to make them new men and women. Say 'yes' to that offer and you're voluntarily allowing God to make you a fit citizen of his eternal kingdom which Jesus called 'my Father's house'. Say 'no' and God allows you to take the consequences of your own choice. D. H. Lawrence said that the awful result was the 'sheer horror' of being 'a god-lost creature' and he, Lawrence, was certainly not a Christian. C. S. Lewis, another great writer (and a Christian), spoke of God who 'in his mercy made the fixed pains of Hell that misery might be stayed'.

HORROR

To Lewis, the Christian, there was an agreed price for refusal to accept Christ's offer. Christ called it 'Hell' in the very bluntest of terms. To Lawrence, the unbeliever, there was only the awfulness of a never-ending, soul-scraping, nothingness.

The New Testament is, of course, quite explicit. To refuse God or to ignore him is to cut yourself off _for ever_ from all that is perfect and best. The choice is a free one to be made here in this life. The results of that decision will be final. You can't go back on it when the Judgement comes. You can't go back to the shop and ask to change the goods because you don't like what you've bought. It's a fearful thought and so it should be.

But if it all sounds rather harsh, remember that it isn't God who wants people to choose to refuse. His offer of eternal life is free and open to all. You have all your life in which he is willing to hold that offer open to you. After all, justice demands that because you're imperfect you should be found guilty. Yet, still, cleansing and forgiveness is there for you and the hope of an eternity of tremendous joy. What a party God has in store for his family! The Bible calls it a wedding reception. So you want to be there? Well it won't be God's fault if you finally miss the party because **the invitation is already sitting there on the mantelpiece waiting for you to reply to it**.

PARTY TIME

So, for those who accept the invitation, there's a marvellous party in store. Try a different picture. God is offering you citizenship of his perfect heavenly city—a lively and satisfying community of peace, justice and love. Centred on God himself, it will be throbbing with joy and creativity. Or just forget the pictures. What really matters is that Christ called the whole thing 'life'. There used to be TV ad which said, 'It looks good, it tastes good, and, by golly, it does you good.' Well, God's advertising agency could beat that any day.

So only a fool would want to miss the party.

I don't want to be that kind of fool.

The Graduate

THE Graduate was probably one of the cinema's all time great films. It collected awards all round. Dustin Hoffman was the hero, Katharine Ross the heroine, Anne Bancroft the baddy. Simon and Garfunkel wrote the memorable music. Have you seen it? You can get it on video. In the film Benjamin comes home from college loaded with prizes, honours, success, achievements, and a head stuffed full of knowledge. But one thing is wrong. He is petrified with indecision. He's learnt it all, and he has no idea what he's supposed to do. None of the knowledge he's gained seems to have equipped him with the ability to decide for himself. What he really lacks is experience—the experience which only comes from commitment. So he just drifts along, inwardly ashamed of himself.

DECISION TIME

The turning point in the film comes when he falls in love with Elaine, a girl whom he's known for years. He wasn't much interested in her, but, under pressure from his parents, he agrees to take her out. Very soon he decides to marry her (long before asking her) and from that moment on he stops drifting and becomes decisive. He is in love and he has a goal. There are plenty of ups and downs after that before 'boy gets girl' but from the moment of decision he is a new person.

Could you be another Benjamin? You've nearly finished this book, you've cracked the God-code, you've got your head full of knowledge about Christianity, you know where it's at—but you've never deliberately committed your life to Christ, never fallen in love with him, never known the experience of wanting to be one with him, never consciously started out on 'the yellow brick road', never accepted the party invitation.

'Narrow,' said Jesus 'is the gate that leads to life, and the way is hard. Few find it.' And right now you may be, in your mind's eye, standing at that gate. Push it and go in. That's what Jesus told would-be followers to do.

OPEN UP!

There's lots of picture language in the New Testament. It's full of gates to be opened, knockers to be knocked, dirt to be washed away, corpses to be raised, new births to be experienced and so on. Each picture helps a little but the idea behind them all is that something really *new* has to begin. So, when I turn to Christ and ask him to remake me, that's when it all starts. My knock has been answered, I'm through the gate, I'm on the road, I've been re-born, I'm clean, I'm alive!

Benjamin was a new person with a new goal when he decided that he wanted to marry Elaine. Yes, but that's just a story in a film. Quite a story, but only a story.

Starting out with Christ—now that's different. That's for real!

'If you've been badly burned you make sure you stay away from the fire in future.'

'Burned—is that how you see being in love?'

Liz's hands clenched tightly on her spoon. 'Who brought love into this?'

'You did. That is what you're talking about, isn't it? Love—and marriage.'

'Ideally, marriage is supposed to be sharing, each person giving equally, but it never happens that way.'

'Giving.' Richard echoed the word softly with a strange intonation that Liz was unable to interpret. 'It isn't just that, Elizabeth, marriage should be give and take, and——'

'Give and take!' Liz winced at the shrill, defensive sound of her own voice. 'You're talking in ideals again. Oh, I know that's how everyone imagines it will be, but it usually ends up with one partner doing all the giving and the other all the taking.'

Books you will enjoy
by KATE WALKER

RUNAWAY

When Rowan ran away from her home and her past, she was catapulted headlong into the life of the unsuspecting Nathan Kennedy. The attraction between them was obvious, and Nathan wanted to help her, but how could she tell him the truth, knowing it would ruin everything?

THE GOLDEN THIEF

Leigh Benedict, superstar, seemed to think every young aspiring actress was a pushover for the casting couch, and his cynical attitude appalled Jassy. But the attraction that flared between them was making it difficult for her to convince him otherwise . . .

GIVE AND TAKE

BY

KATE WALKER

MILLS & BOON LIMITED
ETON HOUSE   18-24 PARADISE ROAD
RICHMOND   SURREY   TW9 1SR

First published in Great Britain 1991 by Mills & Boon Limited

© Kate Walker 1991

*Australian copyright 1991
Philippine copyright 1991
This edition 1991*

ISBN 0 263 77033 8

*Set in Times Roman 10 on 10½ pt.
01-9103-60320 C*

Made and printed in Great Britain

For Steve

CHAPTER ONE

SOMEWHERE in the distance a church clock was striking the hour as Liz rounded the corner and slowed abruptly, the sound of her footsteps dying away as she froze, instinctively huddling into the shadows of a nearby wall, her eyes drawn to the spot where, on the opposite side of the square, light from the wine bar spilled out on to the pavement.

He wasn't there!

Only now did she admit to herself that, deep down, she had never really believed that this meeting would actually take place. Such things weren't part of her world. Blind dates, carefully arranged trysts, with time and place planned to the last detail, were the stuff of romance—and romance was something she had done with long ago. It didn't fit with her newly ordered routine, her rational, businesslike approach to living. Romance stormed through life like a howling gale, wrenching things from their apparently secure moorings, and leaving them lying crushed and devastated in its path when it had gone—as it always went. It never lasted, it was just a temporary aberration, not worth the pain it brought in its wake.

'I knew this was a mistake!'

Liz muttered the words out loud as if actually hearing them would convince her of what she had known all along, but at the same time some small, irrational part of her mind gave a tiny twist of disappointment at the thought that the man she had come to meet, the man with whom she had communicated only by letter for the last six months, wasn't here as he had promised.

So had he never planned to come at all—which didn't fit with the number of times he had suggested that they

7

meet—or was the reason for his non-appearence more simple and practical—just that he was late?

And that was something she understood only too well. How many hours in the past, in what she now thought of as her other life, had she spent waiting, clock-watching, her unease and irritation growing with every second that passed? Only then she had waited in antici-pation, her heart lifting at the sound of a car drawing up in the street outside, her whole being concentrated on the moment when a key would be inserted in the lock, and the door would open. It was only later that she had come to see how she had put her own existence on hold, lost in the joy of loving—loving too much, she now realised.

Or had *she* got the time wrong? Suddenly a prey to doubt, Liz hunted in her handbag and pulled out a folded letter.

No, there it was in black and white. 'Raffles Wine Bar at eight o'clock. I'm looking forward to it.' Well, he hadn't been looking forward to it enough, damn him! If he had, he would have been here by now.

Deep down, she knew that she had never really expected that he would turn up, had told herself that she was only going along with this out of curiosity, that she wouldn't care if he wasn't there—she would treat herself to a meal anyway and not spare him a second thought. But that very rational decision had faded now, washed away on a tide of pure emotion, of anger, un-certainty, and something perilously close to bitter disappointment.

'I'll give him five more minutes,' she muttered to herself. 'Five minutes—no more!'

And even that was too much. She had wasted enough of her life waiting for a man—a man who had been central to her world but in whose life she took second place—to his work.

Liz shifted uneasily from one foot to another, the chill from the pavement reaching her through the thin soles of her elegant black suede shoes. Even though she had convinced herself that Richard Deacon would never keep their date, she still hadn't been able to resist the impulse to dress up for the evening ahead of her, struggling with an irrational urge to wear one of her newest and most flattering outfits, and her final choice, a burgundy silk tunic and skirt suit, was little protection against the autumn cold even though she wore a fine cream wool jacket over it.

Restlessly she lifted a hand to push through her hair, dropping it again hastily as she remembered that her long black mane was coiled into a neat chignon at the back of her head—the change of hairstyle a last-minute decision, one made because tonight she wanted to look coolly elegant and sophisticated, as different as possible from the woman she had been a year ago.

Behind her, the clock struck the quarter-hour, its sound bringing home to her that she had given Richard Deacon more than twice the five minutes she had allocated him and yet she was still standing here, getting colder by the minute—waiting in spite of her private vow that never again would she let this happen to her.

'A quarter of an hour is hardly the end of the world.' A voice from the past sounded in her head, followed by her own sharp reply.

'It is when I have a thousand and one things to do— and eight people due here for dinner any minute!'

No. She didn't want to go through with this. Her first response had been the right one. This whole idea was a mistake and she had no intention of taking it any further. She had managed perfectly well without a man in her life for many months now, and she planned on continuing to do so. There was no room for such complications in her ordered existence.

But even as she turned on her heel, meaning to hurry away, she couldn't resist a glance back to the opposite side of the square, her footsteps faltering as she saw a dark, masculine figure emerge from a side-street and head towards the wine bar with swift, purposeful strides.

'If you want me to wear a carnation in my buttonhole and carry a copy of *The Times* in my left hand, then I will,' he had written in his last letter. 'But I don't think we'll need anything like that.'

And of course Liz didn't need any such way of identifying him. She would have known at once who he was, even if he wasn't the only man standing outside the wine bar, a swift glance at his watch revealing that he had come there for an appointed time, for a meeting—a meeting with her!

Well, he was too late, she told herself, turning away again. But her earlier resolve had weakened and she was frankly stunned as a sudden wave of what she could only call regret washed over her at the thought of leaving him like this.

That illogical feeling was just the result of a guilty conscience, she rationalised. Everything she had ever been taught about courtesy and good manners protested at the idea of arranging a meeting with someone and then letting them down at the last minute, simply because she hadn't the nerve to face them. It was a cowardly, underhand way of going about things, and her inner morality wouldn't let her do it. Besides, if she didn't appear, what was to stop him going round to her flat to find out what had happened?

Liz sighed, acknowledging that there was only one thing she could do. She still didn't want to go through with this date, but if nothing else she had to meet him face to face and tell him her decision, not just turn and run. She owed him that much at least after all those letters——

'Elizabeth!'

The sound of a voice calling her name made Liz wheel round, her heart suddenly racing. Her earlier movement had betrayed her, drawing his attention. He hadn't moved, he was still standing on the edge of the pavement, but now he was looking straight towards her, his eyes narrowed against the darkness.

'Elizabeth?' he said again, less certainly this time.

Liz knew that she had no alternative but to go forward, and although she told herself that this was what she had decided on after all she found that her legs were strangely unsteady, making her steps hesitant and uncertain. He must have seen her turn, must know that she had considered leaving without even speaking to him.

Throughout the short journey across the square she was supremely conscious of the man's eyes on her, dark, disturbingly intent pools in his shadowed face. What was he thinking now that he had actually seen her? They had never exchanged photographs—such things hadn't seemed necessary—so how would he react when they finally came face to face?

As she crossed the road, Liz caught sight of her own reflection in the plate-glass window of a shop and for a second hardly recognised it, the unaccustomed severity of the new hairstyle throwing her cheekbones into sharper relief, making them look thinner, more hollowed, her almond-shaped grey eyes large and dark above a narrow face that was now drawn tight with the tension that firmed her soft mouth so that she looked older than her twenty-six years. Older and wiser, she would have said, but was unable to hold back a rush of loss for the girl she had once been; the girl who had believed in love at first sight and had been bitterly disillusioned. Was it really just the awkwardness of the moment that had etched those lines on her face, or had past events put them there?

'It *is* Elizabeth, isn't it?'

The slight unevenness of the man's voice, a touch of something that sounded like barely controlled laughter, made her wonder if he could be as nervous as she was. He had taken several steps towards her, his hand coming out in greeting, then slowly dropping to his side again as he saw the uncertainty in her face, and Liz too suddenly found herself gripped by a nervous desire to laugh.

He must *know* who she was. Even if he hadn't been sure at the beginning, her response to his use of her name would have told him that she was the woman he had arranged to meet. But he had agreed that they would meet as strangers, the six-month-long correspondence put aside in this new beginning. It would be as if they were completely unknown to each other—and that was just how she wanted it.

All the same, she still felt a small stab of pique at the thought that he could have any doubts about her identity when she had known him from the moment she had laid eyes on him.

'Richard——' That tiny sting of disappointment made her voice uneven. 'Richard Deacon?'

'Who else?'

His smile flashed on and off with the speed of a neon advertising sign—a gesture, nothing more, a token sign of friendliness, but carefully restrained and somehow distant, as if the glimpse he had had of her attempt at retreat had frozen any more warm impulses before they had had time to form.

'Or do you make a habit of meeting strange men like this?'

I don't make a habit of meeting *any* men! Liz wanted to retort, but she caught the words back hastily. If this was to be a new beginning for her, she had to put the past aside, not bring it with her, its shadows and unhappiness casting a blight on the present. And the future? She wouldn't let herself think about that.

'I——'

Disturbed by the mocking quality of his tone, Liz found herself at a loss for words, and irritation at the way he had kept her waiting and her own uncertain response still pricked at her, made worse by the fact that he had offered no hint of an apology. Her unsettled frame of mind was aggravated by the way that, now that she saw him clearly at last, she couldn't drag her eyes away from his face.

He might have had doubts about her identity, but *he* was just as she had pictured him—or at least so much that minor details didn't matter. Perhaps she had thought of him as rather taller. In her two-inch heels she was exactly his height so that their eyes met on a level, which she found disconcerting because of the watchful force of his gaze, his eyes, of the changeable blue-green of a winter's sea, studying her closely from under thick black lashes. His face was more finely carved, too, hard and lean like his body, with a straight nose and firm, deter-mined mouth and chin. The dark hair that sprang around his head in soft curls was closely cropped, giving an impression of a stern, no-nonsense approach to life that, illogically, only made her want to imagine him as a younger, freer-minded man, someone who had once smiled and laughed easily and often, to judge by the fine lines feathering out from his nose and mouth.

There was no sign in that face of the man whose letters she had so enjoyed, no sign of the light, dry humour that on occasions had made her laugh out loud. She would never admit it to anyone, least of all Eleanor, his sister, who had been responsible for the suggestion that they write to each other in the first place, but during the last few months those letters had come to mean a great deal to her, each one read over and over again, and always with the same enjoyment.

But communicating with someone through the im-personal medium of a letter, and meeting them face to face, were two very different things; even as one part of her mind was admitting to an immediate tug of at-traction towards the man before her, another, distinctly uneasy part was wishing that she had never agreed to this meeting. Now, with him actually standing before her, she wanted to go back to that strange, uninvolved relationship they had had as penfriends so that she could simply imagine him as she read his words. Seen in the flesh, he was too real, too physical, too masculine, in a way that made a sensation like cold pins and needles shiver over her skin.

'Look, let's start again.'

His voice told her that he had sensed her unease, and Liz was grateful for his obvious consideration, his attempt to make her relax.

'I'm Richard Deacon——'

He kept his tone carefully formal as once more his hand was proffered in greeting, more determinedly this time, and he didn't let it drop to his side even when, still unable to make the move that would result in actual physical contact with him, she simply stared at it.

It was an attractive hand, her mind registered absently; long, fine-boned like the rest of him, but strong-looking all the same, the fingers square-tipped, nails immaculate. This was the hand that had written those letters, the fine, precise script covering the pages that were carefully stored away in a drawer in her dressing-table, some illogical impulse driving her to keep them though common sense told her she would be wiser to destroy them. She had been tempted to burn the first one without answering it, but there had been nothing in it to upset or disturb her, and the gentle humour, the witty, absorbing account of the small day-to-day details of his life had fascinated her so that, in spite of herself, she had pushed aside all her doubts and scruples and, after several days of resolving not to answer, had finally scribbled a short, non-committal note. That had been the start of it.

'And you're Elizabeth Neal.'

'Liz——' It came out on a gasp as, suddenly becoming aware of how foolish she must look, she pushed her own hand forward and took his. 'Please call me Liz.'

For the first time in almost a year, the name sounded as alien to her as when she had first started to use it, rejecting the other shortened form of her name as too childish and inappropriate to her new position in life.

Liz Neal fitted better with her role as a single career woman; a woman who was making her own way in the world with a successful job, a smart, if small flat, and a whole new approach to life; a woman who had been through the dark times, through loneliness and despair, and who had come out the other end—if not exactly smiling, then at least coping.

'No one ever calls me Elizabeth.' Except my mother, she added privately, closing her mind to the fact that there had once been someone who had used a very different form of her name.

'Liz it is, then.'

But she had caught his faint frown, the slight hesitation before he spoke, and it set up a sensation like the fluttering of a thousand butterfly wings in her stomach, a feeling that intensified as she realised that Richard Deacon still held her hand in his, his fingers warm against hers.

The moment of physical awareness was so intense that for a second she was tempted to snatch her hand away, wrenching it from his grasp as if those long fingers had been the exposed ends of an electric wire that were burning into her skin. But a moment later she regained her grip on herself and even managed a smile as she gently eased her hand away, then ruined the effect completely by pushing it thoughtlessly into her coat pocket as she might have done if she had actually been stung and wanted to protect the injury from the cold night air.

'I——'

'Shall we go in?'

Their two voices, hers unnaturally high-pitched, his low and calm, clashed together then they both fell silent again, Richard smiling an apology, Liz biting her lip in confusion.

'It is awkward, isn't it?' Richard went on after a moment, his smile slightly wry. 'I've never been on a blind date before—and, even after all those letters, I suppose that's really how we have to describe this. I suppose this is how people must feel when they've been brought together by some dating agency and they meet for the first time.'

'Exactly like this.'

That lop-sided smile had been singularly attractive, drawing a tiny curve of Liz's own lips in response. She found it comforting to think that this man who at first sight had looked so self-confident, so totally in control, should feel as uncomfortable as herself. Well, almost as uncomfortable, Liz amended painfully. He couldn't be carrying with him the backlog of unhappiness, loneliness and despair that, even after nine months, still blighted her life—and he hadn't been kept waiting as she had.

'Look, why don't we go inside? I think we'd both feel better after a drink.'

'Oh, but——'

Now was the time to tell him that she had changed her mind, that she wasn't going to take things any further but had only crossed the road to explain that she wasn't going through with this 'date'. But, strangely, Liz found that the words wouldn't come. That boyishly wry smile, and the unspoken admission of unease that had come with it, had thrown her off balance mentally, and she was no longer sure what she was going to do.

The thought of a drink was appealing. She had had a hectic day, she was cold and rather tired, and the interior of the wine bar looked attractive and inviting. She didn't have to stay for the meal Richard Deacon had originally suggested, but it would be gauche and ill-mannered to rush off now. After all, he had come a long way to meet her.

'All right.'

In spite of her efforts to the contrary, her reply sounded stiff and grudging, and once more Liz caught the way Richard's brows drew together in a swift frown. Immediately an unreasoning wave of annoyance washed away the tension that had gripped her.

What had he expected? That she would fall into his arms as soon as they met—and all on the strength of a couple of dozen letters? It would take far more than that to convince her that he was different. She had enjoyed his letters and, honesty forced her to admit, had come to look forward to them, but anyone could profess feelings on paper that they didn't actually possess in real life, and experience had taught her the dangers of trusting too easily. She had rushed blindly into one relationship in the past and had lived to regret it bitterly. She had no intention of falling into that trap again.

'But I'd like to make one thing clear. I want to pay my way. This isn't exactly a date as such—and even if it were, I'd still insist that we split the cost. I'm earning a good salary——'

'And you're a very independent lady.'

A dark, sardonic note threaded through Richard's words. He hadn't liked that, Liz reflected. Her declaration had clearly stung his male pride. All the better then that she had made her position plain from the very beginning. She didn't want him jumping to any mistaken conclusions.

But as she saw his face harden she couldn't suppress a pang of regret at the loss of the caring, sympathetic man who had come across in his letters. Now she knew just why she hadn't wanted to see him in reality. She had built up an idealised picture of him in her mind, and she hadn't wanted that image shattered, shown to be the delusion it must be.

'You make it sound like an insult.' Liz's inner conflict made her tone bitter.

'Not at all,' Richard returned smoothly. 'Independence is a thoroughly admirable trait.'

His tone made it sound exactly the opposite, Liz thought grimly, torn between anger and a wincing sensation of distress at the ice in his voice.

'It's just that I think you'd do better to make sure that your prized self-sufficiency is actually being

threatened before you spring to its defence. Now——'
He moved to open the door, a distinctly unnerving glint
in those blue-green eyes challenging her to object to *that*.
'Shall we go in?'

And that was her put firmly in her place, Liz reflected
as a firm grip on her arm gave her no choice but to co-
operate and move into the light and warmth of the bar.
Perhaps she *had* over-reacted, seeing insults where none
was intended; but then again, how had she expected
things to be? She had come here to meet a man whose
letters had intrigued and delighted her, nothing more.
She couldn't really believe that one meeting would erase
her unhappy past, wipe away all her bitter memories and
change her attitude towards men from one of cynical
suspicion to a deep, abiding trust in one split second.
She knew better than that.

'Can I take your coat?'

Richard didn't add, 'Or would that threaten your independence?' but he didn't have to, the words were implicit in the ironical reflection he used, making Liz grit
her teeth against the angry retort that almost escaped
her. She could afford to be gracious on this, she decided, meaning simply to acquiesce gracefully. But as
Richard's hands came out to ease the cream jacket from
her shoulders his physical closeness brought a sudden
rush of memory that had her tensing instinctively,
shrinking away from him, her face losing colour and her
eyes very wide and dark.

'What the hell——?' With an obvious effort, Richard
caught back his angry exclamation. 'Liz, I am not going
to hurt you. I only want to take your coat.'

For a long, taut moment it was as if they were in a
film that had suddenly stopped, frozen in time with his
hands still halfway towards her. Then abruptly Liz realised how foolish she was being and gave herself a small
mental shake. She had promised herself that she wouldn't
bring the shadows of the past with her tonight, but it

seemed that the memories were not going to be as easy to shake off as she had believed.

'I'm sorry...'

But all the same she hastily shrugged herself out of her jacket before he could help her, handing it to him awkwardly, keeping him always at arm's length, her heart thudding painfully as she saw the way his mouth had firmed to a thin, hard line, his lips compressed against whatever he had been about to say. He took unnecessary care over arranging her coat over the back of a chair as if needing time to collect himself, swallow down the anger her reaction had sparked off in him. His own navy overcoat was more speedily dealt with, before, clearly once more fully in control, he turned a politely enquiring glance in her direction.

'I'll get the first round.'

Liz steeled herself to ignore the gentle emphasis on 'first'; petty sniping wasn't going to get them anywhere.

'What would you like to drink?'

'Campari and soda, please.'

There was a perverse sort of delight in knowing that she'd surprised him. Because he knew about her childish sweet tooth, the last thing he would expect her to choose would be such a bitter drink. But her tastes had changed lately. Perhaps she was growing up at last—and about time too, a painfully realistic part of her brain added disconcertingly. She had come very close to making a total mess of her life by rushing into things with the impetuousness of a five-year-old.

'Won't be a minute.'

Privately, Liz hoped he would be rather longer than that. She needed some time to herself, to sit quietly and adjust to the situation in which she found herself. She had thought earlier that this meeting hadn't turned out to be quite what she had expected, but the truth was that Richard Deacon himself was the unexpected element in all this.

Liz's mind went back over the letters she had received, acknowledging that in among the gentle wit and delightful accounts of his life there had been just a faint thread of the determination she had seen stamped on his face earlier. Over most of the major issues on which he had expressed an opinion, his attitude had been tolerant and scrupulously fair, but it had also been clear that he didn't suffer fools gladly—and she had had a taste of just what that meant already.

Perhaps things would have been easier if he hadn't made it so obvious that he was trying so hard. Liz sighed faintly, wondering how other people managed this sort of situation. But then very few others would find themselves in this particular scenario. The closest anyone might come to it would be those clients of a dating agency that Richard had mentioned. Her mouth twisted in a wry grimace as she recalled the advertisements she had seen: 'You too can find love!' 'Lonely? Desperate? Not any more! With Kindred Spirits you can find the love of your life.'

But that wasn't why she was here. Love wasn't what she—or Richard Deacon, for that matter—was looking for. Once, a long time ago, it seemed, when she had been another person, she had thought that she had found what the purple prose of those advertisements called the love of her life. She had been convinced that her future was all mapped out for her, certain that, no matter what the statistics on marriage and divorce might say, *this* relationship was one made in heaven, one that would last forever. But love was blind, they said, and in her case that had been so very true. For a few short years she had lived in a dream world, an idyll of happiness, but then it had all turned sour, and she had no desire to risk going through all that ever again.

So why *was* she here? That was a question Liz didn't find easy to answer. Because Richard had asked her to come and she had been unable to resist her overwhelming curiosity about the man who had written those wonderful letters, she decided. But somehow the thought of mere curiosity didn't satisfy her. It wouldn't satisfy her mother either, she admitted to herself. Jane Neal wasn't the sort of person to bemoan her daughter's single state. A divorcee herself, she was a staunch advocate of female liberation, believing that any woman was perfectly competent on her own, and scornfully dismissive of the idea that she needed a man in any way. She had always maintained that Liz had a strong—or, in her mother's opinion, a weak—romantic streak in her make-up, one that left her too readily a prey to the spurious attractions of the opposite sex. That might have been so—had been so once, Liz admitted—but not any more.

'One Campari and soda.'

Lost in thought, Liz started nervously at the sound of Richard's voice, hastily composing her features into a carefully polite smile as he set her drink down on the table in front of her.

'I hope you wanted ice.'

'Oh, yes—that's fine, thanks.'

Lifting the glass, Liz took a hasty sip of the cool, tart liquid, hoping that the alcohol would ease the tension that tightened her muscles as he lowered himself into the chair opposite her. He was being ultra-careful again, the restrained politeness of his tone reviving all her unsettled feelings at once. Perhaps that was what was wrong. They were pussyfooting around each other like two people who had been forced together by circumstances beyond their control, who were going through that infernally awkward stage of trying to get to know each other, not daring to put a foot wrong because they were obliged to spend the evening together.

'Look, I'm sorry I was late.'

Richard had obviously used the time he had been at the bar to think and had come to the conclusion that it was only his lateness that was making her so stiff with him.

'But I——'

'It doesn't matter,' Liz jumped in quickly, too quickly, she realised ruefully, catching once again that quick, disturbing frown that revealed a side to this man that was usually hidden behind the smiling, urbane exterior. 'I wasn't exactly on time myself.'

Try as she might, she couldn't make the words sound convincing. They came across as petulant, resentful of his belated apology, and instinctively she tensed, waiting for Richard to react, illogically feeling worse, not better, when he simply reached for his drink murmuring, 'Well, I *am* sorry.'

It would have been so much more honest—and easier—if Richard had lost his grip on the flash of temper she had seen barely in control when she had insisted on paying her share. If they could have had an argument, however irrational, it might have cleared the air—and at least they would have been saying what they really felt instead of this awkward side-stepping of any possible cause of dissent that made her feel as if she were walking across a tightrope stretched high above a yawning cavern.

And that feeling was all the more disconcerting because, illogically, she had never expected it. It had been so easy to communicate with the man who had written those letters. In her own replies the words had simply flowed on to the paper. In fact several times, on re-reading what she had written, she had torn her letters into tiny pieces, astounded by the depth of feeling and intimate details she had revealed about herself, before rewriting them in a more restrained form.

But, as she had already told herself, it was one thing to pour out her soul to a man she couldn't see, a man she believed she would never meet, quite another to sit with him only feet away from her, his long legs disturbingly close to her own under the wrought iron table, and try to make some sort of conversation.

And she had to say something. Richard seemed to have drawn in on himself, leaving it up to her to make the first move.

'Did you get the Roper Foundation contract?'

For a moment the sea-coloured eyes looked curiously blank as if her question had been the last thing he had expected, but then after a moment he recollected himself.

'As a matter of fact, we did. The final papers were signed this afternoon—I've come straight from there.'

Which probably explained his lateness. It also explained the dark grey formal suit, crisp white shirt and expensive silk tie. Recalling her own indecision about what to wear, Liz hadn't expected such elegance for a meeting that was 'just to break the ice'—but, of course, it hadn't been for her but for his business meeting.

'You've driven from Nottingham tonight?'

As Richard's glossy dark head inclined slightly in agreement, Liz struggled to bring her voice down from its high, sharp pitch.

'That's a heck of a trip—you should have said. We could have changed the date—arranged to meet some time when you weren't quite so busy. I wouldn't have minded.'

Wouldn't you? Her mind threw the question at her unexpectedly, forcing her to face the fact that, if he had tried to change their arrangements, she would probably have minded quite considerably, taking it as meaning that he had had second thoughts and was trying, tactfully, to put her off. But, equally, she wasn't sure she liked the idea of being something of an afterthought, tacked on to his day—relaxation after a tough business meeting. That smacked rather too much of the sort of thing she had only just escaped from.

'I didn't know things were going to be finalised quite so soon.' Richard's voice had hardened perceptibly in response to her tone, not her words. 'It was no problem—though I have to admit that I would have liked a chance to freshen up—change into something more comfortable.'

Which meant that he wouldn't have worn that suit this evening if he'd had the choice. Would she have felt less uneasy if he *had* been more casually dressed? Liz wondered, trying to imagine him in less formal clothes and not finding it easy, which was strange because whenever she had pictured in her mind the Richard Deacon who had written those letters, the image she had had of him had been one of a more relaxed figure, someone in jeans and a sweater perhaps. But now, seeing him in that immaculate suit, which had clearly been tailored to his exact measurements to judge by the perfection of its cut and fit, and in which, in spite of his comment about changing into 'something more comfortable', he looked completely at ease, she found it hard to imagine him dressed any other way.

'But you must be tired——'

'Not at all. I have a good car and I enjoy driving—it gives me time to think.'

A perceptible hesitation before his final statement made Liz pause to think too. Just what had he wanted to think about on the journey? Had he too had his doubts about this meeting, had he perhaps, like her, considered calling the whole thing off, having weighed his promise to her against the demands of his work? It was what she had half expected, after all.

Belatedly, Liz recalled that her original intention had been to tell Richard that she wasn't staying, that only politeness had made her agree to having a drink with him. But after what he had just told her she was glad that she had agreed. To have let him drive all the way here from Nottingham for no purpose would have been crass and selfish. And he *had* decided to come after all, she told herself, swallowing down her earlier pique.

'So celebrations are in order.' She lifted her glass in what she hoped looked like a light-hearted toast. 'Congratulations!'

No answering smile lightened Richard's expression. Instead of the pleased triumph she might have expected to see in his face, there was a sombre, thoughtful look that was disconcerting and inexplicable.

'Thank you.' Once more his dark head moved in acknowledgement. 'I thought I'd get it, but all the same it's good to have everything finalised.' There was no arrogance in his tone, only the confidence of a man who knew he was good at his job and took pride in the fact. 'The competition was pretty tough—it's a hell of a big project.'

He had relaxed noticeably now, leaning back in his chair, glass in hand, launched on to a topic in which he was interested and about which he knew a great deal.

'It's a challenge to create something that will serve the function it's intended for and yet won't clash with its surroundings. Anything too modern would look terrible with all those wonderful old buildings near by.'

'But your work would never create any problems like that!'

Blue-green eyes met grey swiftly, Richard's slightly narrowed as if in surprise at her comment.

'The papers were full of praise for the riverside development you worked on,' Liz continued hastily, not wanting to admit that she had made a point of learning as much as she could about the things he had achieved over the past year. It was a strange situation, she reflected, knowing so much about Richard and yet not really knowing *him* at all. Even if he had never written to her, it would have been difficult to be unaware of the impact he had had on the world of architecture. In spite of his comparative youth—he was only four years older than Liz herself—he had already gained a reputation for brilliant, innovative ideas that were combined with a strong respect for the timeless elegance and beauty of buildings from other centuries so that, whether he worked on shopping centres, office blocks, or, as in his award-winning venture, a huge leisure complex, the end result was always graceful and beautiful, blending in perfectly with its surroundings, creating something that was as pleasing to the eye as it was efficient and functional.

'I enjoyed designing that,' Richard said simply. 'Though I have to admit that I had to fight for what I wanted. The monstrosity they originally had in mind would have stuck out like a very sore thumb indeed—a great lump of concrete and plate glass, totally obscuring the view of that wonderful old town hall from the opposite side of the river. I see my job as trying to get people to look at things as a whole, not just their own tiny little part of it. It'll be the same with this new project——'

Enthusiasm got the better of politeness as Richard launched into a clear, concise explanation of his aims. To Liz his words seemed to blur inside her head as she watched him sketching invisible buildings in the air or mapping out his plans on the glass top of the table before him. She found herself mesmerised by the confident movements of those long, fine-boned hands, noting subconsciously the contrast between the impression of delicacy in the elegant, flexible fingers and the hard strength she had felt just for a moment when he had led her into the bar.

She could picture those hands at work on a drawing-board, skilfully sketching out the shape of the buildings he saw in his mind. It would be wonderful to watch. A *frisson* of awareness shivered over her skin as she had a sudden heady vision of what it would feel like to have those same hands on her body, to know their skill, their strength, their delicacy, used for a very different purpose.

Heat flooded through her veins as her eyes went to the absorbed face of the man before her, her gaze lingering on his mouth, and she was unable to stop herself from imagining how those lips would touch her own in gentle caress, growing more demanding as passion rose in both of them. How long was it since she had been kissed in that way? How long since she had been held in strong, masculine arms, felt the brush of hard finger-tips over the sensitised nerves of her skin? How many nights——?

Dear lord, what was she doing? Shock made Liz sit up stiffly as she stared sightlessly at the opposite wall. How could this have happened? How could she have let her mind wander on to things she didn't want to remember? She wanted to *forget* such things completely, forget that she had ever felt such passion, ever loved enough to give herself body and soul to a man, putting aside her own needs for his sake, driven to distraction by the wild flare of desire that his touch, his kisses had aroused.

She wanted to forget! Over the past nine months she had endlessly tried to put such thoughts out of her mind, but now, when it was the last thing she wanted—the worst thing that could happen—she was forced to remember the foolish, irrational passion that had made her rush into the worst mistake of her life—her marriage.

CHAPTER TWO

'I'M SORRY—I'm boring you——'

Noticing Liz's sudden abstraction, Richard had misinterpreted the reasons for it.

'No—really——'

The tingling awareness of her body, the rush of blood to her head, made it difficult to speak with any conviction. She knew from his frown that he hadn't believed her, and his words confirmed that opinion.

'I do apologise. When I get involved in something I forget that not everyone is as enthusiastic about architecture as I am.'

Already hypersensitive and on edge as she was, Liz wished that he wouldn't make it quite so obvious that he was hunting for some way of changing the topic of conversation, looking for something that wouldn't bog them down in the deeper matters neither of them was ready to pursue.

'I think it's only fair that you have your turn now. Tell me about yourself—what are you working on at the moment?'

'A biography of Balzac,' Liz responded automatically. 'It's going to take me ages to get through it—it's huge—full of quotes and footnotes, and the language is so complex it needs careful work to get the translation exactly right.'

As she spoke she thought she knew exactly how he had felt earlier, why he had taken up the subject of his own profession with such enthusiasm. Work was a safe, neutral topic, like the weather, Christmas, or where you were going on your holiday, the sort of thing everyone resorted to when trying to talk to someone they didn't know. In the back of her mind she recalled an article about how to make friends which she had once seen in a magazine. 'Ask questions—about the other person's work, for example,' it had exhorted its readers, and as she responded to Richard's questions about her own job as a freelance translator Liz couldn't suppress a wry inner smile at the thought that the author of the article would be proud of both of them—they were following her advice to the letter.

'And when you've finished that—have you anything else lined up?'

'No, after that I'm free. I thought I'd probably take a break for a week or so then—have a holiday.'

Holidays—another safe topic, possibly second only to the weather. The author of 'How To Make Friends' could use this conversation as a perfect example of just the sort of thing she had meant. And Liz was glad to get off the topic of work. A lingering worry about the way she too had relaxed when talking about her job shed a new and disturbing light over events in the past, one which had to be pushed to the back of her mind so that she could concentrate on the present as she had determined to do.

'Have you thought where you'd like to go?'

That wasn't easy to answer. You were wrong, Liz mentally addressed the writer of the magazine article. Holidays aren't as neutral a topic as you think. Because the truth was that she had thought long and hard about the question of where she wanted to go on this, the first holiday she'd taken on her own for years, but somehow nothing appealed. The places she had always wanted to visit or go back to were now shadowed by memories that it hurt to recall. Venice and Rome were where she had spent her honeymoon, Moscow, which she had always longed to see, was forbidden territory because it was where she would have gone next if her marriage hadn't broken up, and Durham, which she loved so much, would bring every agonising memory rushing back.

'Oh, just somewhere warm and sunny.' She didn't care if her lack of conviction showed in her voice; she just wanted to get off this subject that was severely undermining her composure. 'It's been so cold and miserable lately, you wouldn't believe it's only just October!'

She was really scraping the barrel now, talking about the weather, and, to judge from his expression, Richard thought so too. Liz anticipated some satirical comment on that point, but to her relief none came.

'Would you like another drink?' he said instead.

A pointed glance drew her attention to her glass which, Liz noted with some surprise, was already empty. She had no recollection at all of drinking anything, and the alcohol had done nothing to calm the restless, jittery feeling that still had her in its grip.

'No, I don't think so, thanks.'

'Then are you ready to eat?'

Now was the time to say that she wasn't staying—that she had only agreed to have a drink with him because she had felt obliged to. But Richard had already turned, lifting a hand to draw the attention of a waiter.

'To tell you the truth, I'm ravenous,' he admitted with a smile when menus had been provided and they had been left to make their choice. 'I had lunch in Nottingham but that must have been—oh, eight hours ago.'

Once again Liz was forced to push her plans for a hasty retreat to the back of her mind. She could hardly back out now, leaving him to eat on his own. Besides, she was hungry too, she realised with some surprise. Earlier, her stomach had been so churned up with tension that she would have sworn that she wouldn't be able to eat a thing, but now the appetising smells that wafted into the bar from the restaurant made her mouth water and she studied the menu with an unexpected enthusiasm, one that increased as her eyes lighted on a particular item.

'Oh, great—they do lasagne! I haven't had that for...'

Her voice died away as she glanced up, meeting those blue-green eyes head on, and a rush of memory closed her throat. It had been on her honeymoon that she had started her love-affair with Italian food. There hadn't been much money to spare, so they had dined as cheaply as possible, and as a result Liz had become hopelessly addicted to spaghetti, pizza and lasagne which, with its savoury filling and rich cheese sauce, had always been a particular favourite.

'Elizabeth——'

'I think I would like another drink after all,' Liz said hastily, her voice raw and unsteady.

For one dreadful moment she thought that Richard might push her to explain what was wrong, press her with questions she couldn't answer, but after a swift, searching look at her colourless face and over-bright eyes he got to his feet at once.

'Of course—same again?'

Liz could only nod silently, incapable of remembering her earlier insistence that she should pay her share. She only wanted him out of the way, wanted to be left in peace for a moment in order to collect her thoughts— but peace was the last thing those thoughts brought, so she closed her eyes against the pain that tore at her. It seemed as if she could actually taste the tangy flavour of lasagne in her mouth, feel the hot Italian sun on her skin, and she almost believed that if she opened her eyes she would see, not the busy, crowded bar, but the smiling face of the man she had once loved so desperately.

'Beth——'

'*No!*'

Liz's eyes flew open, her hands coming up before her face in a violent gesture of panic and rejection so that if Richard hadn't stepped back hastily they would have caught the glasses he held and sent them flying.

'I told you—my name is *Liz*!'

She couldn't bear to hear the sound of that other, shortened version of her name, the one she had rejected completely when she had walked away from her marriage. Hearing it again like this, spoken in a voice that was low and filled with concern, brought back bitter memories of the times she had heard it spoken in another, very different voice, one husky with passion.

'I'm sorry.'

Richard set the glasses down on the table with a distinct crash.

'I'm sorry,' he repeated. 'I didn't mean——'

'My name is Liz,' Liz managed through gritted teeth, the effort of holding back the pain that tore at her tightening every muscle in her face.

'Of course.'

The force of her reaction had startled him; she could hear it in the over-precise crispness of his tone, his own jaw suddenly as stiff as her own.

'I'm sorry. I'm afraid Liz isn't a version of Elizabeth that I like very much. I've always preferred B——'

A warning flash from Liz's grey eyes made him bite off the end of the offending word, and in the awkward silence that followed he lowered himself into his chair, pushing her glass towards her with one long forefinger.

'Have some of that—it'll make you feel better.'

Liz wished there were some way she could raise the glass to her lips without actually having to pick it up. The tremor in her hands was all too obvious, betraying the way she was feeling inside, as she gulped down a couple of hasty mouthfuls of her drink without a thought for the possible lack of wisdom of her actions, feeling a tiny sense of relaxation, a slight thinning of the fog inside her head, as the alcohol took effect. Richard sat quietly, watching her, waiting a nicely calculated moment before he spoke.

'Do you want to talk about it?'

'No!'

Liz stared fixedly at her glass, not daring to turn her head to face him. She knew he was studying her closely, could feel those changeable eyes fixed on her so intently that she felt sure her skin must burn where they rested, but she couldn't bring herself to meet that searching gaze. If she did then he must surely read her distress far too easily.

'No, I don't want to talk about it.' Cold and hard with the effort of maintaining some degree of composure, the voice she heard sounded quite unlike her own. 'As a matter of fact, what I really want to do is to go home.'

'Oh, no.'

Quietly, almost gently spoken, the words still had an underlying thread of steel that turned them into a forceful response, one that broke through the rigid control Liz was imposing on herself and brought her head up in a swift, involuntary movement, grey eyes locking with blue over the top of her glass.

'No,' Richard repeated. 'I'm not letting you go home in this state. You look as if you might pass out at any moment. You're going to stay here and finish that drink, and then——'

'Are you ready to order now, sir?'

Liz's hand jerked convulsively, spilling some of her drink, as she started in surprise at the waiter's interruption. She had been so intent on Richard and the things he was saying that she hadn't noticed the man approaching their table. Immediately Richard leaned forward to take the glass from her hand and set it down on the table.

'Yes, quite ready,' he continued so smoothly that it was as if the revealing moment had never happened.

No! Liz tried to make her tongue form the word. Her unexpected appetite had vanished as swiftly as it had come, and now she couldn't eat a thing. She would choke if she tried to swallow so much as a mouthful. But her throat had dried completely, the husky croak that was all she could manage totally inaudible—or at least, if he did hear it, Richard simply ignored it and proceeded to give his instructions to the waiter.

Through the buzzing haze in her head, Liz was vaguely aware of the fact that he was ordering a meal for her too. *Not* the lasagne, that much registered on her dulled brain with a rush of relief, but simple, straightforward English food that would bring no bitter memories with every mouthful. She could only feel a deep thankfulness that, with innate tact, Richard had ignored her earlier enthusiastic outburst. Even the smell of the herbs that were so much a part of Italian food would make her feel ill, she was sure.

But a moment later that relief was replaced by a sudden rush of anger at the realisation of how high-handedly Richard had ignored her declaration that she wanted to go home. He had even reverted to the old-fashioned, macho way of ordering for her, without even asking what she wanted. The flare of fury cleared her head so that when the waiter had gone she turned on him, grey eyes flashing fire.

'How dare you? If I wanted a meal, I'm perfectly capable of ordering it for myself. I——'

'You didn't seem capable of anything,' Richard put in coldly. 'And it's not a question of *if* you wanted a meal—you're having one. You look as if you haven't eaten properly for weeks.'

'I need to watch my weight,' Liz responded swiftly, wishing desperately that every word she said didn't revive memories of her marriage. She had been much plumper then, her childhood sweet tooth always getting the better of her, no matter how hard she tried to resist temptation.

'If you don't eat anything, you won't have any weight to watch,' Richard commented drily. 'Anyway, I invited you here for a meal, and a meal you're going to have— so finish your drink and we'll go through to the restaurant.'

Belatedly, Liz suddenly remembered the conditions she had laid down earlier, and, reaching for her handbag, she pulled out her purse.

'It was my round,' she said harshly. 'This should cover it.'

For a long, silent moment, Richard stared at the coins she held out, his expression disturbingly blank as if he had just been slapped in the face so hard that it had stunned him. Then abruptly he let his hand fall open, palm upwards, some inches away from her own so that she was forced to move to let the coins drop into it.

'Thanks.'

The single syllable was curt and sharp as he pocketed the money without even looking at it before reaching for his glass and draining what was left in it in one quick swallow.

'Are you ready?' he asked, leaving Liz no option but to agree as he was already on his feet.

'Ready' was definitely not the way to describe the way she felt, Liz reflected as, reluctantly, she followed him towards the dining-room. This was probably going to be one of the most awkward and least enjoyable meals of her life, second only to the dinner she had had on the last night of her marriage when she had known deep down that the only option open to her was to leave, but she hadn't had the courage to admit it, even to herself, until later events had pushed her into action.

But, this time, Liz was pleasantly surprised. By the time they were both seated, Richard seemed to have thrown off the dark mood that had descended when she had insisted on paying for the drinks and set himself to being polite and charming company, launching into a discussion of a play they had both seen recently, a love of the theatre being something they both shared, something that had often been mentioned in the letters that had passed between them. Slowly Liz found herself relaxing, responding to his questions with a growing ease, even offering one or two of her own until the conversation flowed between them with a lightness that she had never anticipated.

She must have eaten too, though she couldn't actually recall having done so, because after a time she found that when the attentive waiter came to take her plate it was completely empty, every morsel cleared from it.

'Something from the sweet trolley, madam?'

Automatically, Liz was about to refuse, but then a particular dish caught her eye, making her mouth water.

'Oh, yes—profiteroles, please.'

Richard had been lounging back in his chair, staring down at his hands, but now his head came up sharply and he shot her a swift, questioning glance. Shaken by the disturbing intensity of that look, the way it seemed to probe into her mind, searing over already hypersensitive nerves, Liz flashed him a wide, over-bright smile.

'I've decided not to watch my weight tonight,' she declared in a voice that was too high-pitched for comfort, the tension that had gripped her in no way eased by the way his eyes held hers for a moment longer then flicked to the waiter, a tiny, almost imperceptible shrug of his shoulders dismissing the matter from his thoughts as he refused a dessert for himself, choosing cheese and biscuits instead.

This was just what she needed, Liz told herself as she felt the rich, sticky chocolate sauce melt on her tongue with a sensual pleasure. As a child she had had a real problem with her weight as a result of turning to sweet things, eating for comfort, when the rows between her parents had become too intense for her peace of mind. But years of careful control meant that her size was no longer a problem so she could afford to indulge herself every now and then. And if her enjoyment of the rich sweet didn't fit with the sophisticated career-girl image she had originally wanted to present tonight, well, so what? She was enjoying herself at last.

A sudden burst of laughter from a nearby table drew Liz's attention to a group of young people, and one girl in particular who, with a happy glow in her eyes, a flush of colour on her cheeks, was ripping the paper off a brightly wrapped parcel with the enthusiasm and lack of restraint of an excited child.

'It looks as if someone's having a good time,' Richard murmured quietly. 'What is it about a present that brings out the child in all of us?'

Something in his intonation caught on Liz's nerves, destroying her new-found pleasure in the evening. It was impossible not to recall all the presents she had received from her husband, small ones at first, then, as their financial situation improved, larger, more lavish, more expensive ones—presents that had brought her no pleasure because they had been bought only for show, like elaborate wallpaper pasted over crumbling, rotting plaster, an attempt to disguise the fact that their marriage was already disintegrating rapidly.

'Almost all of us,' she said tartly, digging her spoon into the profiteroles with unnecessary force, and hastily lifting another sweet spoonful to her mouth. But her enjoyment of the dessert was ruined, the chocolate sauce suddenly cloying and sickly, and she couldn't help remembering the first time she had ever eaten this particular sweet, the memory reviving all the feelings of unease and uncertainty she had experienced on that first visit to her mother-in-law's perfect home.

'Most people like presents,' Richard continued with a peculiar emphasis, and Liz was grateful for the fact that her mouth was so full that he couldn't possibly expect an answer.

She fully anticipated that he would pursue the matter further, and found herself tensing in apprehension, but instead his next words changed the subject so dramatically that at first she couldn't believe she had heard him right.

'Why did you agree to meet me, Elizabeth?'

How did she answer that? Liz wondered, swallowing the last of her mouthful with a nervous gulp. And *Elizabeth*, she noted. He didn't like Liz and she had forbidden him to use the other, more emotive version of her name.

'You—you asked,' she managed with difficulty.

An abrupt movement of Richard's hand dismissed her inane comment impatiently. 'I asked you to meet me at least half a dozen times before, if you remember, and you always refused. So, tell me, why did you agree this time?'

Because of the things Eleanor had told her? Because the bitter memories of her marriage had faded at last? Because she knew that she couldn't hide away forever, she had to face the world some time? Liz considered the possible answers to Richard's question and rejected them all as not quite accurate. The truth was that she didn't really know why she had given in to his last request for a meeting when she had rejected all the others out of hand.

'Your letters intrigued me,' she said at last. 'I wanted to meet the man who had written them.'

It wasn't the answer he wanted; she knew that by the way his lips compressed into a hard, unyielding line. What *had* he expected? she thought on a wave of anger. Did he, like so many other men, believe that because she had been on her own for a while she must be desperately frustrated, that she must be missing the intimacies of married life so much that she would welcome any man's attentions in their place?

'I thought it would be nice to talk——'

'Talk!' Richard broke in harshly. '*Talk!* If that's what you wanted, you haven't exactly done it! You've barely said a hundred words that mattered all evening—and I had to drag those out of you!'

Suddenly he leaned forward, elbows on the table, his hands clasped tightly and his sea-coloured eyes burning into hers so that she flinched back from the force of their gaze.

'Do you really want to *talk*, Elizabeth?'

Liz's heart had taken up an uneven, jerky rhythm, one that made it impossible to breathe naturally so that her breasts rose and fell rapidly under the rich-coloured silk of her suit, and as she saw Richard's eyes darken rapidly she could be in no doubt that he was well aware of her reaction.

Suddenly she was gripped by a powerful and totally irrational sense of betrayal as she stared at the hard, implacable set of his face, some powerful emotion turning his eyes as dark and disturbing as the North Sea on a winter's day. What had happened to the man in those letters—the gentle, caring, tolerant man she had wanted to meet? *This* Richard Deacon was none of those.

But at the same time some tiny, irrational part of her brain was registering the forceful beauty of those deep-set blue-green eyes, the power of that sculpted face, recalling the warmth of his smile, the way those lips, when they weren't so tightly compressed, looked full and sensually inviting. It had been so long since any man had kissed her, so long since she had felt the warmth and strength of a hard, masculine body close to hers. Her own body felt unnaturally hot, glowing as a result of the heated blood that coursed through her veins, and her throat was painfully dry, her heart racing.

Dear lord, what was happening to her? Was it true then that once a woman had known a man's lovemaking she was an easy victim of her own need afterwards? Before tonight, Liz would have rejected that idea out of hand, but now she was no longer so sure.

'No——' Her voice croaked embarrassingly and she swallowed hard to ease the discomfort in her throat. 'No, I don't want to talk. As a matter of fact, I think I'd better be going—it's late——'

A belated glance at her watch told her that it was nothing of the sort. It was barely half-past ten. She had spent little more than two hours in this man's company, and yet she was exhausted, emotionally limp as a damp cloth that had been wrung out. She felt as if she had run a marathon and then been subjected to a particularly savage form of brainwashing—and yet all Richard had done was to be charming, pleasant company.

She should never have come. She should have left without speaking to him as she had intended to at the beginning—or at the very least after that first drink. She had known that meeting him tonight would be a mistake, and she had been proved right. The past still haunted her, her memories too painful, still too close to the surface, to allow her to relax in any man's company, particularly Richard Deacon's.

From the way Richard's mouth twisted in response to her declaration, she anticipated some scalding retort and hastily bent to pick up her bag in order to hide her face, freezing in mid-movement at his surprisingly quiet and totally unexpected response.

'Can I see you again?'

Very slowly Liz straightened up, her fingers clenching round the small, envelope-shaped bag as if it were some completely inadequate lifeline.

'Another date? I don't think——'

She broke off abruptly at his harsh crack of laughter.

'Another *date*!' Richard gave the word a darkly satirical emphasis that made her toes curl inside her smart suede shoes. 'Elizabeth, sweetheart, this was no date! It was more like a summit conference—the sort the superpowers hold to decide whether they're going to talk to each other or not. If we were going to have a proper——'

'Well, we're not going to!'

Liz's mental and physical exhaustion seemed to have reached even the bones in her body so that they ached with the effort of simply sitting upright. All she wanted was to get out of here as quickly as possible—and she could only pray that her legs would support her when she stood up.

'We're not taking this any further, Ri——'

She couldn't say his name, not when he was looking at her in that way, with his eyes almost black with some emotion that she couldn't put a name to, and his face looking as if it had been carved from granite and weathered by a fierce, northern wind.

'I don't want to see you again. This—I——' Her tongue stumbled over the words in her anxiety to get them out. 'This isn't going to work. It was a mistake—so let's say goodbye now and leave it at that.'

She was sure that he would argue with her, and her heart quailed inside at the prospect of having to find the words to resist him, but then the heavy lids hooded his eyes and he folded his hands together with unnatural precision.

'Goodbye, Elizabeth.'

Stunned by his sudden and unexpected capitulation, Liz could only stare in disbelief, not sure that she had heard him right. The silence that descended seemed to stretch out interminably, drawing her nerves tighter with every second that passed, until suddenly Richard looked up again, his eyes like blue-green ice, meeting her troubled gaze with a frightening lack of emotion.

'*Goodbye*, Elizabeth,' he repeated more emphatically, his freezing tone bringing her to her feet in a rush.

It was too late for second thoughts, Liz told herself as she made her way awkwardly out of the bar and into the cold darkness of the night. And, besides, such thoughts were foolish, dangerous—and yet there had been times during the evening when she had come close to liking Richard Deacon very much—too much for her own peace of mind.

No, she told herself firmly. She had said that their meeting tonight was a mistake and she had meant it. If she had seen it as a chance to begin again, exorcise the ghosts of the past—and by now she was past knowing just *how* she had seen the prospect of meeting Richard—then it had failed miserably. The wounds left by her marriage were too raw, not fully healed, and tonight's experience had simply ripped off the fragile, protective covering that had begun to form over them. It had all been a terrible mistake—one she was never likely to want to repeat.

CHAPTER THREE

FROM the moment she woke the following morning, Liz knew that the profiteroles—or, at least, the rich chocolate sauce that had covered them—had been the wrong thing to eat. Her night's sleep, slow as it had been in coming, had meant that she had missed the usual warning signs that preceded an attack, but she needed no such advance warning now. The painful throbbing of the right side of her head meant that she was already in the throes of a particularly bad migraine.

'Oh, *why* did I weaken?' she groaned aloud, not daring to open her eyes yet, knowing that even the dull light of the morning would be painful.

On other occasions she had managed to get away with eating chocolate with no ill effects, but that particular trigger food, when combined with the stresses of last night, had produced a devastating effect. She wouldn't be able to work at all today, she told herself ruefully, trying to resign herself to the stretch of wasted—and painful—time ahead of her; in fact, she probably wouldn't be able to do *anything*.

With an effort she forced her eyes open, wincing sharply as she did so. What she needed now were the tablets the doctor had prescribed. They would at least take the edge off the pain, though they usually worked so much better if she could take them before the attack was as established as this was.

Her footsteps slow and dragging, she made her way into the bathroom and wrenched open the medicine cabinet, staring in shock and dismay at the empty bottle on the glass shelf. Of course, she had run out a couple of weeks ago and had meant to ring the doctor for a repeat prescription but had never got round to it.

Liz slammed the cupboard door shut, grimacing at the noise it made and in distaste at the pale face, shadowed with a sickly tint of green, that stared back at her from the mirror. Phoning the doctor was easily done, but then she would have to go down to the surgery to collect the prescription—and that was something she wasn't looking forward to at all, not when every movement set her head spinning and made the appalling throbbing even worse. With a despondent sigh she wandered into the living-room again, sinking down into a chair and closing her eyes against the sickening waves of pain.

Half an hour later she was still there, feeling far too rotten to move. The phone call to the doctor had been made, but when she tried getting to her feet the room swung round alarmingly and she didn't trust herself out in the street, let alone at the wheel of her car. On the opposite side of the room, the piles of papers, dictionaries, and the word processor on her desk seemed to glare at her in reproach, but tackling the complicated translation of the life of Balzac was the last thing she could cope with right now. All she wanted was to crawl into some dark hole and close her eyes.

The sound of the doorbell seared through her head like a scream, making her groan aloud and bury her face in her hands. She didn't want to see anyone, couldn't face the effort of making even the slightest attempt at conversation. But whoever was at the door clearly had no intention of going away again as the bell reverberated through the room once more, making Liz feel that the soundwaves it produced were an actual, solid, physical force pounding against her temples. Wearily she got to her feet, grateful for the fact that at least she had managed to pull on some clothes, even if they were only a black sweater and cord jeans, their funereal colour matching her mood.

'I'm coming!'

Her weak shout was ineffectual—no one could have heard it through the thickness of the door—but Liz didn't dare to raise her voice. Even the slight effort she had made had left her feeling as if the top of her head had been blown off, a situation that was not at all helped when the bell rang again.

'All right, don't be so impatient!'

With luck it would just be the postman, or someone else she could get rid of quickly. Liz prayed it wasn't Mr Penman, the old man who had the flat upstairs; she couldn't cope with his endless need for a chat today.

But when she opened the door it was to find the last person she expected—or wanted—to see standing outside. Richard Deacon was in the hallway, his hand half raised to press the bell once more. Liz stared at him through blurred, unfocused eyes.

'What are you doing here?' she demanded ungraciously.

'Good morning, Elizabeth.'

The mild reproof in his tone she might have anticipated, the smile she most definitely did not. It seemed too bright, too open for this time in the morning, particularly after the way she had left him the previous night, and she almost felt that, like sunshine, it would hurt her sensitive eyes.

Richard looked very fresh, alert, very vital and alive, with the glow of some time spent in the crisp autumn air on his skin, his blue eyes clear and bright, exactly the opposite of the way she was feeling. He was dressed in the same superbly tailored dark grey suit as the day before, his immaculate appearance in stark contrast to her own wan pallor and sombre clothes. Liz knew she looked like death but she couldn't bring herself to care.

'I thought you'd gone back to Manchester.'

'That was my original plan, but last night I—realised that I'd had rather too much to drink to be safe driving so I booked into a hotel for the night.'

Which was all very reasonable—in fact, eminently sensible, Liz had to admit—so why did she feel suddenly nervous and strangely threatened?

Because he was *here*, the answer came back sharply. Because he hadn't just checked out of his room and gone on his way as she might have expected after that uncompromising 'goodbye' last night. And he hadn't had too much to drink when she had left him—she was sure he'd been perfectly sober. So what had happened after she'd gone?

'And?' she said, knowing that there had to be an 'and'.

Richard's grin did disturbing things to what little composure remained in her aching head.

'And I thought I'd call round to see if you'd changed your mind about another evening together.'

She should have known! Men! Give them half an inch and they took three hundred miles! But she had thought that after the way they had parted last night he would leave her in peace.

'Have you?'

Unable to speak, Liz unwisely made a move to shake her head violently then instantly regretted it as the room swung round her and she grabbed at the door for support, holding it so tightly that her knuckles showed white.

Immediately Richard's attitude changed, his eyes narrowing swiftly as he took a step forward, his hand coming out to her.

'Elizabeth, what's wrong?'

A searching glance took in her white face and clouded eyes, the way her hand had gone to her forehead.

'Migraine,' he pronounced firmly. 'The profiteroles, I suppose?'

Liz could only scowl ferociously. He was far too perceptive for comfort, but by now she was past caring. She just wished that he would go and leave her alone. Any minute now, if things followed their usual pattern, she was going to be violently and disgustingly sick, and having Richard present when that happened was a humiliation that she couldn't bear. Even in the intimacy of marriage, she had always kept such moments strictly private.

But Richard showed no sign of leaving. Instead, he moved into the room, both hands reaching out to grasp her by the shoulders, not hard, but firmly enough to prevent any resistance if she had felt capable of making it—which she most definitely did not.

'Sit down.'

Quiet though his voice was, it held a note of command that she would be a fool to ignore, and Liz allowed herself to be manoeuvred into the living-room and into a chair where she leaned her head back against the cushions with a sigh of relief.

'Have you taken anything?'

Was his tone really as sharp as it sounded, or were her ears, too, as oversensitised as the rest of her head?

'I—I ran out. I've phoned the doctor and he's leaving me a prescription at the surgery.'

'His name?' Richard rapped out. 'The address?'

Unthinkingly, like a tired child, Liz gave him the information he wanted.

'Right—I'll see to the tablets—as for you, it's time you were in bed. Can you make it all right, or shall I carry you?'

'No!'

That was the last thing Liz wanted. She had no doubt that he could pick her up and carry her quite easily, but the thought was more than she could bear. For a brief, agonising moment she had an intense image in her mind of a scene from her wedding-day, heard a voice saying, 'Well, wife,' before strong arms had picked her up and, in the time-honoured tradition, carried her across the threshold of their house, through the living-room—and straight up into the bedroom.

'No.'

In an unwary move she leapt to her feet then reeled desperately, moaning in pain.

'Beth!'

Liz was beyond noticing Richard's use of the forbidden form of her name; her stomach was heaving and she knew that what she had dreaded most was now inevitable.

With a strength she hadn't known she possessed, she pushed Richard out of her way and dashed towards the bathroom door. She didn't hear him follow her, only knew that, as she leaned over the sink, only just reaching it in time, a warm hand came to rest on her shoulder and another gently lifted the hair back from her forehead.

'All right——' His voice was low and soft, infinitely soothing. 'All right, sweetheart—don't fight it—just relax.'

He could have spared her this! Liz thought wretchedly. He could at least have had the tact to stay away! But a moment later she was grateful that he hadn't as Richard reached for a flannel, holding it under the warm water tap for a short time before wringing it out and wiping her face with it as tenderly as a mother would care for a sick child. It felt so good that she simply closed her eyes and enjoyed the sensation, no longer caring who he was or why he was there.

'Better now?' Richard asked at last. 'Do you think you can make it to your room or would you rather stay here for a while?'

In spite of herself Liz couldn't hold back a tiny chuckle at the way he had phrased his question.

'I can think of other places I'd rather be,' she managed shakily. 'The Bahamas for one, or——' She stopped abruptly, wincing painfully because her weak attempt at a laugh had hurt so much.

'Or in bed,' Richard finished for her in a tone which brooked no further discussion of the matter.

He made a move as if to pick her up bodily, then hesitated, obviously recalling her earlier reaction and thinking better of it. Instead, he held out both his hands to her and when she put her own into them eased her gently to her feet, tightening his grip to steady her when she swayed weakly.

'Come on, let's get you tucked up, then I can fetch those tablets for you.'

'It's all right——' Liz protested feebly, the words coming out in a gasp as his arms slid round her shoulders, warm, supportive, and infinitely comforting—*too* comforting for her peace of mind because all she wanted to do was to lean back against their strength, rest her head against the firmness of his chest—and that would be a very foolish move indeed.

'No, it isn't all right,' Richard snapped, mistaking the reasons for her reaction. 'You can't think I'd let you go out in this state.'

That was the last thing on her mind, Liz thought hazily, the pain in her head momentarily pushed aside by her response to Richard's physical closeness, the faintly musky scent of his body, the warmth of his touch. She was suddenly overwhelmed by a weak longing to cuddle closer, feel his arms fold round her, their strength enclosing her, and the struggle to resist the impulse was almost more than she could cope with. Her free hand fluttered upwards, moving towards Richard's face. If she could just touch him...

Her fingers were within an inch of his cheek when Richard flinched back sharply as if he had been stung, and the hand that enclosed hers tightened painfully.

'Bed!' he said curtly. 'You're almost out on your feet as it is.'

He half supported, half carried her towards the bedroom, and Liz was deeply thankful for his help, feeling she would have collapsed in a limp heap at his feet if he had let her go. But bitter tears stung her eyes as she cursed that moment of foolish weakness, praying

he would take it as just the result of her illness. That
had to be the answer, she told herself. She couldn't think
of any other reason for her behaviour.

A few moments later she was in her room, watching
as, one-handed, Richard pulled down the blankets that,
unable to face making the bed properly, she had simply
yanked up roughly earlier that morning, before he turned
to survey her, a strange, opaque cloudiness in his eyes.

'Wouldn't you be more comfortable——?'

Liz knew only too well what he was about to suggest,
and her feelings must have been written on her face as
she saw his expression close up in response.

'Well, I'll leave that up to you,' he said gruffly. 'I'll
get you a drink.'

With her own moment of inexplicable weakness still
uppermost in her mind, Liz made very sure that she was
in bed with the blankets pulled up close around her by
the time Richard came back, even though the rush to
strip off her jeans and sweater and pull on a nightdress
had made her head pound sickeningly. For one dreadful
moment she had thought that he might suggest un-
dressing her himself, but to her surprise he had backed
down much more swiftly than she had anticipated,
leaving her a prey to a feeling that in any other circumstances she would have called disappointment. But there
was no possible reason for her to feel that way now, so
it couldn't be that.

She had only been in bed for a few seconds when
Richard returned carrying a glass which he set down on
her bedside table.

'Only water,' he told her. 'I don't want you being sick
again.'

Of course he didn't. It had been an extremely un-
pleasant experience for her, and Richard Deacon must
have found it positively distasteful. The women he
usually dated would be as sleekly sophisticated as he was;
he would never see them in such abject, humiliating distress—in fact, they were probably the type who were

never caught with a single hair out of place, except, perhaps, in bed. Liz caught in her breath sharply as something stabbed deep inside at that thought and Richard heard the slight sound, his dark brows drawing together in a frown.

'You need those tablets inside you. I'll go and get them now. I'll be as quick as I can.'

'Don't hurry on my account.' Liz managed a feeble attempt at humour. 'I'm not going anywhere.'

Her words stopped Richard on his way to the door.

'You will be all right?' There was a new sharpness about his voice, one that made her hasten to reasure him.

'I'll be fine.'

She didn't care if 'fine' hardly described the way she felt, it was time she asserted some sort of control over the situation. She appreciated Richard's help, but that didn't mean she was going to let him take over.

'I'm quite capable of looking after myself.'

'It looks like it,' was the sardonic rejoinder before the door swung to behind him.

Liz's main feeling at seeing him go was one of overwhelming relief. Pain was pounding at her temples, and although she knew that the chocolate she had eaten on the previous night was probably what had triggered the migraine attack, she also strongly suspected that tension had a great deal to do with it too—tension that was the result of the thoughts and memories that just being with Richard had woken in her, and which had been growing stronger with every minute that had passed since she had opened the door to find him standing outside. But, all the same, she was glad that he'd come. She couldn't have faced the prospect of walking the couple of miles to the doctor's surgery—because there was no way she would have been safe to drive—to collect her prescription herself.

With a sigh she leaned back against the pillows and closed her eyes, trying to ignore the pain in her head and make her taut muscles relax. It was a strange feeling, leaving everything in someone else's hands, particularly a man's, and it was one she had never experienced before. Her father, in the few short years she had known him, had never been the sort of man to help in the home in any way and she had soon learned, like her mother, that if something needed doing she should get on and do it herself. And during her marriage she had always had more than enough to cope with. Everyone had told her how hard it was to combine the pressures of a job— because then she hadn't been working from home, but had been employed by a large business conglomerate, translating their foreign correspondence and contracts— with the demands of being newly married, but she simply hadn't listened. Hopelessly in love, she had laughed at the thought that perhaps she had taken on too much, and, in the beginning, things had been fine. She had enjoyed the challenge, prided herself on being supremely organised, and it was only later——

No! With an effort Liz dragged her thoughts back from the path they were following. Remembering those days was a mistake. It did no earthly good at all, but simply brought home to her afresh how she should put the disintegration of her marriage out of her mind and start anew, with her mother's example as her inspiration. After all, Jane Neal had been in a far worse situation, abandoned by her husband with a young daughter to care for—and she had had no career to fall back on, having married straight from school, but had been forced to take any job that was offered simply to keep a roof over their heads.

She didn't know if she dozed or simply let her mind go mercifully blank, but either way the sudden, intrusive sound of the living-room door opening startled her into wakefulness. She hadn't heard the car returning and Richard had been far quicker than she had ever anticipated. He must have driven like a bat out of hell to get to the surgery and back in so short a time.

Perversely and irrationally, because she knew she needed the tablets, Liz wished he had stayed away longer so that she could have had more time to adjust to the alien situation in which she found herself. Having to rely on a man so completely made her unsettled and restless, and yet it was comforting too.

Richard's footsteps were approaching her bedroom door and, suddenly painfully shy, Liz closed her eyes hastily as he came into the room.

'Elizabeth? Are you asleep?'

Slowly and reluctantly she opened her eyes again and looked up at him, the reality of her situation coming home to her with a sudden sharp intensity as she registered the dark, masculine force of his presence in the once secure haven of her bedroom so that, disturbingly, she felt her eyes burn with tears. Immediately concern flooded his face.

'Is it so very bad?' he asked, the gentleness of the question severely threatening her already precarious self-control.

She was suddenly convinced that he was going to come to the bed and take her in his arms and she wasn't at all sure how she might react to that. But then he seemed to hesitate, and when he continued it was in a very different, much more businesslike voice.

'I've brought the tablets, they should help.' He shook two of the capsules into his palm, lowering himself on to the bed at her side as he held them out to her with a fresh glass of water. 'Get these into you quickly. Is the light bothering you?' he asked, seeing the frown that was her attempt to fight back the betraying weakness of her tears.

It's not the light—it's you, Liz was tempted to retort, but he had already moved to draw the curtains over the window so she swallowed down the reply with the tablets, grimacing as one stuck in her strangely tight throat. Hastily she gulped down the rest of the water.

'Thanks.'

It came out on a shaky gasp. The effort of sitting up
had set off the terrible throbbing in her head again and
she pressed her hands to her temples, all colour draining
from her cheeks.

'Lie down!' Richard commanded sharply, and automatically she obeyed him, closing her eyes and biting
her lip against a moan of pain. Dimly she heard
Richard's muffled curse and his sudden movement as he
came to sit beside her again. 'You must feel rotten.' One
hand stroked the limp dark hair back from her face with
infinite gentleness. 'Poor Beth——'

Through a haze of pain Liz caught the sound of the
forbidden name.

'I told you not to——' she muttered through clenched
teeth, still keeping her eyes tightly shut so that she sensed
rather than saw his mental withdrawal even though his
fingers continued their soothing caress.

'Not to use that name—I know.' In contrast to his
earlier gentleness, Richard's voice now sounded clipped
and distant. 'But you'll have to forgive me—it comes
easier to me than Liz.' Liz shivered as she caught the
cold distaste that hardened his tone. 'And Beth is so
much—warmer——'

But Liz couldn't risk letting him go on. She was
already far too vulnerable, and that softly caressing hand
was weakening her defences even further, making her
feel as if something that had been sleeping deep inside
her was slowly wakening, uncoiling itself, making every
nerve-end come disturbingly alive. With a painful effort
she forced her eyes open to break the spell.

'I'm very grateful to you for all you've done.' It was
a struggle to inject any strength into her voice. It sounded
so weak and drained that he must have had to strain to
hear it. 'But I'll be all right now. There's no need for
you to hang around; you must have work to do——'

'The work can wait.'

Richard dismissed her protest curtly, his hand never
ceasing in its gentle massage of her throbbing temple,

but his eyes were as dark and impenetrable as the sea at night so that she could read nothing of his thoughts in them.

In spite of herself, Liz found that his touch was having an almost hypnotic effect on her, soothing her tension and making her relax slowly. She felt warm and safe and surprisingly at peace.

'The tablets always make me sleepy——' She forced herself to try again.

'Then I'll stay until they work.' Richard's tiny pause lasted the length of a heartbeat, and when he spoke again his voice was lower, huskily intent. 'Unless you want me to go, Elizabeth. If you really don't want me to stay, you only have to say. Is that what you want? If so, tell me that you want me to go.'

The powerful tablets were already taking effect. Liz felt as if she were floating in a warm, calm sea, suspended in time and place as the pain in her head ebbed away, and all she was conscious of was the soothing caress of a warm, strong hand which had now moved to the muscles in her neck, easing away the tension that lingered there. Her eyelids drooped and closed, suddenly too heavy to keep open any longer.

'Richard...' she murmured softly, no longer knowing whether she had meant to inject a protest or dismissal into the word.

'I'm here,' was the quiet response. 'I'm here, Beth, and I'll stay just as long as you need me—if that's what you want. Just tell me——'

What *did* she want? The answer came disturbingly easily—she wanted to stay like this, with his hands caressing her, his lean body so close that she could feel its warmth, inhale his personal scent each time she breathed. Her limbs felt limp and incapable of movement, her pulse slow and relaxed.

'Do you want me here, Beth?' Richard asked. 'Do you want me to stay?'

Liz couldn't find the strength to care about his use of that once dear, now hated name. Sleep was rolling over her like lazy waves lapping a sun-baked shore. She was already drifting away on its warm tide, but just before it claimed her completely she made one last, tiny effort.

'Stay...' she sighed before oblivion claimed her.

CHAPTER FOUR

IT HAD to have been a dream, Liz thought when, hours later, she surfaced slowly from a deep sleep to find herself alone in the darkened room. She had to have imagined it all; Richard couldn't have been here, in her flat, caring for her so generously, taking over her life. She could never have let him do that.

But then her gaze fell on the bottle of tablets standing on the bedside cabinet and, knowing how she had found it impossible to get to the doctor's herself, she had to face the fact that it had been no dream at all but the truth.

And now Richard had gone. She was stunned to find how much that thought distressed her, a pang of disappointment twisting inside her. She hadn't wanted to see him again, had felt that it was dangerous to let him into her life, but at the thought that he was probably miles away by now—perhaps already back in Manchester and out of her life for good—a wave of despondency swept over her, making her mood as grey and dull as a foggy November morning.

'So you're awake.' The quiet voice breaking into Liz's thoughts made her start uncontrollably. 'Are you feeling any better?'

'What are you doing here?'

Too late, Liz realised that she hadn't meant the question to sound as it had; the tartness of her voice that was the result of being startled by Richard's unexpected appearance at her bedroom door was a mistake that she recognised as soon as she saw his finely shaped mouth tighten worryingly.

'You asked me to stay,' he pointed out with icy reasonableness.

57

'I——'

She couldn't have done that, could she? She couldn't have been so foolishly weak. But then she remembered murmuring something as she fell asleep, when, mesmerised by his voice, the touch of his hands, she had foolishly let the barriers down—but never again! It was too risky, far too dangerous. She had come perilously close to getting involved again, which meant laying herself open to the devastation she had experienced before.

'Only until I fell asleep!'

This time, the coldness of her tone was no mistake but a deliberate attempt to push him away mentally, to put an emotional distance between them, but, disturbingly, Richard appeared totally unaffected by her lack of warmth.

'I promised I'd stay until you felt better,' he stated calmly. 'And I always keep my promises. So, like it or not, you're just going to have to put up with my company for a while longer.'

'I feel better now.'

That wasn't strictly true. The blinding pain had eased, but the tenderness around her temples warned her that the headache still lingered, subdued but not eradicated by the tablets she had taken.

'If you mean that you don't look as if you're about to pass out at my feet, then I agree with you,' Richard responded drily. 'But you're far from well yet. These things usually last for twenty-four hours, and, although you've slept for quite a time, you won't be really right until tomorrow morning.'

'You're not——'

Liz swallowed down the instinctive protest as she realised how ridiculous it would sound. How could she declare that she didn't want him to spend the night here, that she couldn't bear the thought of being in bed while he was in her flat, when she had already done exactly that? But somehow the thought of just that situation happening in the dark hours of the night made her heart jolt into an uncomfortably jerky rhythm that brought a wash of colour to her cheeks. She was suddenly supremely conscious of the fact that she was wearing only a white cotton nightdress, even if it was very prim and proper in its Victorian design. She might have felt too ill to worry about such things before, but now that she was thinking straight again she didn't like the situation she was in one little bit.

Richard was in her bedroom, his strong, slim figure suddenly alien and threatening among the gold and white décor, sending a *frisson* of apprehension shivering over her skin. He didn't *look* dangerous, but appearances could be very deceptive.

'I'd like you to leave——'

Liz broke the sentence off abruptly as she saw Richard's dark head move in adamant denial of her request, her mind veering frantically between anger, something dangerously close to panic, and another emotion, one she hadn't felt for so long that she found it hard to recognise. The only way to describe it was— *excitement*. The word fell into her thoughts like a stone into a pond, sending ripples reaching out from it to repercussions which she didn't want to contemplate, making her rush into unguarded speech.

'I really would prefer to be left alone!'

'Tough.' The single syllable was as hard and unyielding as Richard's face.

'But I——'

'Isn't it time you had another dose of pain-killers?' Richard broke in, his voice suddenly bland and smooth again, totally without the hard note that had darkened it a moment before, making Liz blink hard in astonishment at his swift change of mood. 'The instructions on the bottle say two tablets every four hours.'

'Have I been asleep for as long as that?'

Momentarily diverted from her train of thought, Liz glanced at her alarm clock, stunned to find that in fact she had slept for four and a quarter hours. As she had told Richard, the tablets usually made her sleep, but normally only for an hour or two. Last night must have taken more out of her than she had thought.

'And you'll need something to eat. You shouldn't take medication on an empty stomach.'

The fact that Richard was right did nothing to appease Liz's sense of outrage at the way he seemed determined to ride roughshod over her wishes and to impose his decisions on her without a care for what she felt. She had had enough of that in her marriage, she wasn't prepared to tolerate it now.

'I'm not hungry.'

Superstitiously Liz crossed her fingers against the white lie. Now that the sick feeling had abated she felt she could face something to eat, and, if things followed their usual pattern, in a little while she would be ravenously hungry—but she didn't want to make any concessions to Richard.

'And I asked you to go——'

'Nothing too heavy.' Richard blithely ignored her. 'How about soup and toast?'

'Richard!'

Blue-green eyes met grey in a look of total innocence, as if he had no idea what had caused her outburst.

'I can't possibly leave until I know that you're really all right—that you've taken another dose of pain-killers and eaten something.'

'And then you'll go?' Liz persisted, feeling as if she were banging her head against a brick wall but finding herself unable to stop.

'We'll see,' was all that Richard would concede. 'Do you feel well enough to come into the living-room? There's no need to get dressed, just——'

'I'm quite capable to putting my clothes on!'

She would manage it if it killed her, Liz resolved. She would feel far less vulnerable if she was properly dressed. So far, Richard had shown no sign of anything other

than concern for her, but she would be wise not to tempt
fate too far. Or did she mean that she would be wise not
to tempt *herself*? she wondered, remembering her
physical sensitivity towards him during the previous
evening. It was still there now, even under the anger and
resentment at the way he had taken control, a feeling
like the slow smouldering of a sluggish fire, needing only
that tiny extra spark to flare into blazing flames. And
what would provide that spark? A touch, a kiss—or
simply a look—a word? The thought made her feel
burning hot and then shiveringly cold.

'As for food—there's some soup in the fridge—I made
it myself. There's enough for two,' she felt obliged to
add, belatedly realising that Richard had been in her flat
since around nine that morning and probably hadn't
eaten anything in all that time. Courtesy forced her to
offer him something, though she was painfully aware of
the way that her implied invitation would make it appear
that she had gone back on her earlier declaration that
he must leave. They would have something to eat and
then she would insist that he went, she vowed to herself.

'I'll go and heat it up, then. You'll probably want to
freshen up before you eat.'

She needed more than a simple 'freshen up', Liz reflected as she surveyed her pallid cheeks and lank black
hair in the bathroom mirror. She needed a complete
overhaul if she was to look even remotely human. With
her ashen complexion, long dark hair, and an unflatter-
ing touch of redness about her eyes, she looked like
something out of a Hammer horror film. It was no
wonder that Richard had shown no sign of anything
other than concern for her health—no one could find
her at all attractive like this.

Her head came up sharply, making her wince both at
the unguarded movement and the direction in which her
thoughts were heading. She didn't want to make herself
attractive to Richard Deacon! Last night had been a
mistake, and now she just wanted him out of her life.

But, all the same, her pride and self-esteem were severely threatened by the picture she presented. It went strongly against her personal code to appear looking anything but her best.

At least she could wear something better than the sombre black sweater she had had on earlier—*not* to impress Richard she told herself, pulling on a white blouse and a pink lambswool cardigan that threw a little colour on to her face, but to make herself feel better, more able to face the world. The cardigan, which had large black flowers embroidered on it, went well with the black jeans she had worn that morning, and all in all she felt rather more confident as she made her way through the small living-room which doubled as her work-room and into the small, compact, green and white kitchen.

'Nearly ready,' Richard greeted her as he took two slices of toast from the electric toaster and buttered them swiftly. 'Sit down and—I'll see to that!' he interjected sharply as Liz moved to stir the soup which was beginning to bubble.

'It would have boiled over!' she protested.

'I had my eye on it—*sit down!*'

Unwillingly Liz allowed herself to be pushed down on to a chair. It didn't feel at all right to sit back and let Richard do all the work—not that he wasn't obviously perfectly capable—but this was *her* kitchen and he was making her feel as if she wasn't needed, as if she was somehow superfluous and out of things, which was not a feeling she was used to—and one that she wasn't at all sure she liked. To her embarrassment she found herself resenting Richard's obvious competence in preparing the simple meal, which was crazy when she'd always despised men who affected a helpless lack of ability in the kitchen or any other area of domestic responsibilities.

'I'm not dying!' she declared snappishly. 'I'm quite capable of stirring a pan of soup!'

Richard shot her a swift, assessing look before turning the heat off under the pan and pouring the soup neatly into the waiting warmed bowls.

'You don't make things easy for me.' He gave the words a deliberate satirical intonation. 'Why are you always so damned bloody-minded?'

'I'm not bloody-minded—I just value my independence!' Liz declared, anticipating the sardonic way his mouth twisted in response to her outburst.

'I know—we had all that out last night. But, as I said then, do you really think that your prized independence is going to be threatened by letting me buy you a drink or——' he gestured towards the bowls, now brimming with rich French onion soup and emitting a savoury aroma that made Liz's mouth water '—or heating up some soup?'

If he had meant to make her feel small and stupid, then he had succeeded perfectly, Liz admitted rather shamefacedly. She was over-reacting—but the worrying thing was that, instead of wanting to apologise as any reasonable person might, she found herself prickling with hostility.

'I don't like being dependent on anyone!'

'And letting someone prepare you a meal when you're ill is being *dependent*?' Irony rang in Richard's voice. 'For pity's sake, Elizabeth, lighten up a bit! I just wanted to help.'

'And I appreciate that.' Liz felt as if she were on an emotional roller-coaster, swinging up and down with alarming speed as, having made the instinctive concession, she hastened to add, 'But I would have managed fine on my own—once I'd got the tablets.'

The look Richard turned on her seared over her nerves, making her flinch as if she had been burned by a live electric wire.

'You have a real phobia about taking anything from anyone, don't you?' he said harshly, setting the soup bowls down on the table with a distinct crash. 'What is it that scares you so much?'

'I'm not scared! It's just——'

Unable to find the right words, she stirred her spoon round and round in the dark brown soup, her movements abrupt and jerky so that the liquid threatened to spill over the side of the bowl. Richard seated himself opposite her but she couldn't bring herself to look at him so that she jumped like a startled cat when his hand came out to cover her own, stilling the restless movement.

'Just what?'

Liz stared at the long, slim fingers resting on her hand. They were deceptively thin and fine-boned, the strength of his grip told her that, and for a moment she had another vivid image of those hands at work on a drawing-board, using swift, decisive movements to map out clear, precise lines on paper, creating the shapes and configurations that would one day rise into the buildings he had pictured in his mind.

But although her rational mind concentrated on the practical skills in those talented hands, her body was reacting on a deeper, more instinctive level, responding to the warmth and strength of his touch in a way that set her skin tingling, quickening the pace of her heart so that the rush of blood through her veins made her glow inside as if she had just swallowed a large glassful of some potent spirit, throwing her mentally completely off balance.

'It's just?' Richard prompted hardly.

With an effort Liz wrenched her eyes away from his hand, flinging her head up and meeting his searching sea-coloured gaze head on, her own eyes almost black with remembered pain and the struggle to deny what she had been feeling.

'Once bitten, twice shy,' she flung at him and saw his expression change swiftly, something cold and distant sliding down over his face, like blinds being closed, shutting her out. And although she would have sworn

that she didn't want him to feel anything for her she was
stunned by the sharp stab of pain that flashed through
her as his hand was swiftly withdrawn.

'So that's what all this is about,' he said flatly.

'It's not *about* anything! It's simply that if you've been
badly burned you make damn sure you stay away from
the fire in future.'

'Burned—is that how you see being in love?'

Liz's hands clenched tightly on her spoon. 'Who
brought love into this?'

'You did. That is what you're talking about, isn't it?
Love—and marriage.'

'Nothing of the sort! If you remember, you started
this conversation by implying that I had a complex about
being independent. What century are you living in, Mr
Deacon? Women live their own lives now; they don't
need a man to make them complete. There's very little
a man can do that a woman can't manage too. And as
for love——'

The words died on her lips, swept away under a fresh
wave of distress. Love left you too vulnerable, too dependent on the other person.

'And as for love?' Richard repeated sardonically.

'It's definitely overrated. Ideally, marriage is supposed to be sharing, each person giving equally, but it
never happens that way.'

'Giving.' Richard echoed the word softly with a strange
intonation that Liz was unable to interpret. 'It isn't just
that, Elizabeth, marriage should be give and take,
and——'

'Give and take!' Liz winced at the shrill, defensive
sound of her own voice. 'You're talking in ideals again.
Oh, I know that's how everyone imagines it will be, but
it usually ends up with one partner doing all the giving
and the other all the taking.'

She'd angered him, she thought on a quiver of apprehension, seeing the way his eyes had darkened rapidly,
the tautness of the muscles in his jaw. When she expected

a furious outburst, his next words came as a shock that was like a blow to her heart.

'Tell me about your marriage, Elizabeth.'

'No!' It was an explosion of fear and rejection. 'You've no right to ask that—it's none of your business!'

'Why not? I'm willing to tell you about *my* marriage—you've only got to ask.'

They were getting in too deep, swimming in dark, treacherous waters where jagged rocks lurked just below the surface, rocks that were formed from memories, old pain, lost feelings, disillusionment and betrayal.

'I don't want to know——' Even as she spoke the words she knew that they weren't true, the need to know gripping her like a vice, making her voice shake in a way that turned her vehement declaration into an obvious lie. 'If I wanted to see you again, if there was any future for us, then it might be different, but meeting you last night was a mistake, and today——'

She broke off abruptly, knowing a shiver of fear at the way his eyes had narrowed in the cold, hard mask that was his face. Liz was suddenly terrifyingly aware of the fact that she was alone in her flat with this man, a man she didn't really know, and certainly didn't trust. Mr Penman might be upstairs in his flat, but without his hearing-aid he was as deaf as a post, and he was infuriatingly lax about using it. He was unlikely to hear her, even if she screamed.

No, she was letting her imagination run away with her. With a determined effort, Liz pulled herself together, dismissing her fears as the fantasy they were. Richard looked angry, shockingly, coldly angry, it was true, but that was because she had offended his male pride by telling him she didn't want to see him again, something that, in his arrogance, he had clearly never anticipated, but he was unlikely to do anything violent.

'And this morning I wasn't myself. I *did* ask you to leave——' she added with a touch of desperation. It didn't have to be like this. Surely the woman she had become since the break-up of her marriage could tell him that she didn't want to take things any further with more composure and control than she had displayed so far. Such behaviour was too much like the younger Beth, it didn't fit with Liz Neal.

'So you did.' Richard's hard-edged voice cut through her stumbling attempts to get her message across. 'But you're forgetting one thing, Elizabeth.'

Liz's heart sank as she realised what he was going to say. In a moment of weakness brought about by pain and distress, she had asked him to stay, and now he was cold-bloodedly going to use that against her.

'No, I'm not forgetting it! It just has no bearing on anything! I was doped up on the tablets—I didn't know what I was saying.'

'Is that the truth?'

'Of course it's the truth! I *didn't* know what I was saying!'

The ugly scraping sound that Richard's chair made as he pushed it back violently made her flinch inwardly.

'What are you doing?' she cried on a startled gasp as he got to his feet.

'Leaving,' Richard declared succinctly. 'Which, as you've been at such pains to point out, is what you've wanted me to do all along.'

'Oh, but——' Irrationally, now that she had her wish, Liz found that she couldn't just watch him walk out like this.

'But what? You're surely not going to tell me now that you meant it after all when you asked me to stay?'

'N-no——' Liz shook her head in confusion. Right now, she didn't know what she meant at all.

'I thought not.'

Richard swung round on his heel, heading for the door. There had to be a better way to handle things, Liz thought rather desperately. She couldn't just let him go like this.

'Wait! You—I——'

It was so difficult not being able to see his face but only his stiff back, every taut muscle in it speaking eloquently of the anger he felt.

'You haven't finished your meal,' she managed inanely.

Richard turned very slowly, his dark-eyed gaze going to the bowl on the table and then flicking up to her face, and something in his expression brought fiery colour rushing into her cheeks.

'So I haven't,' he drawled sardonically. 'Is this an invitation to stay after all?'

'Well, I don't suppose you've eaten anything for hours, and it would be a shame to waste it.'

'True.'

He was making a great thing about deciding, Liz thought irritably as the seconds dragged past. In another minute she was going to withdraw her invitation, whether he was starving or not!

At long last Richard moved, returning silently to the chair he had vacated so recently, and Liz didn't know whether she was glad or sorry to see him sit down in it again. A disturbing gleam in his eye warned her that he was not just going to give in easily, and, sure enough, after swallowing a mouthful of soup, he turned to face her again.

'This is particularly good soup—and, yes, it would be a pity to waste it—but you've got it all wrong, Elizabeth. The way to a man's heart is not, as popularly believed, through his stomach.'

She was back on the roller-coaster again. Just when she thought they had made a sort of a peace, he came out with a remark like that, making her stomach lurch and irritation prickle all over her like pins and needles.

'It's not your *heart* I care about! I was simply thinking of the time I spent making that soup——'

'Of course.'

The disconcerting gleam in Richard's eyes was more pronounced now, and there was a satirically mocking intonation in his voice that set her teeth on edge.

'Of course I realise that you're used to something very much better than just soup and toast at lunchtime, but it is at least——'

The sudden movement of Richard's hand, clenching over his spoon, made her break off abruptly, and she sensed him bite back an angry retort, his careful control making his words clipped and curt when he responded.

'This is every bit as good as anything I'm used to, especially as it's home-made. I admire you for going to the trouble of preparing it yourself—most people wouldn't bother, they'd just open a tin. But, like independence, some things which are admirable in themselves can become a problem if they're taken to extremes.'

They were back on dangerous ground, Liz thought, feeling very much as if she were in the middle of a mine-field, not knowing if one unwary move would cause something to blow up right in her face. She didn't want to continue this discussion, and so she side-stepped the issue completely, moving on to trivial everyday matters instead.

'Have you seen Eleanor lately?' Surely his sister would be a topic they could talk about without dissension.

For a long, tense moment she thought that Richard wasn't going to follow her lead and change the subject, his frown and the look in his eyes making her heart lurch nervously. But then he gave a tiny, almost imperceptible shrug as if dismissing his doubts and answered reasonably enough.

'She called round briefly the other week—a flying visit, of course—but then you know Nell, she never lets her feet touch the ground.'

Liz nodded silent agreement. She had always envied the way Eleanor Baldwin managed to combine a high-powered job as a literary agent with being a wife and mother of a six-year-old daughter. Richard's sister was always organised, in control, and always immaculately groomed, she thought, one hand going automatically to her limp hair, a pang of distress twisting in her at the thought of how she must look at the moment.

'I don't know how she manages everything. She always seems to do so much—and she has so much energy.'

'Oh, yes, Nell's never been able to sit still for long. She's only happy when she's busy—and Mark's much the same.'

What had put that odd note in his voice? Liz wondered. If she didn't know better, she would have thought that he didn't exactly agree with the way his sister and brother-in-law ran their lives. But that didn't fit with what she knew about his own workaholic tendencies, about which Eleanor had been extremely eloquent the last time they had talked.

'It's certainly hard to find a moment when they're both free—to invite them for dinner or something.'

Liz had started to relax, feeling that the dangerous point had been passed, but, hearing her own words, she tensed up again, recalling all the wonderful dinner parties Eleanor had invited her to and how inadequate they had always made her feel. Like her mother, Richard's sister was a wonderful cook, both women seeming to be able to turn out a cordon bleu meal without the slightest effort.

Richard nodded slowly. He was studying his empty soup bowl as if it were a crystal ball in which he might read the future.

'It wouldn't suit me,' he murmured, referring to his own previous statement as if Liz hadn't said anything in between, and making Liz glance at him in some surprise.

'You wouldn't want your wife to work?'

Richard's head came up sharply, blue-green eyes blazing into hers in a way that made her feel as if she were a rabbit held transfixed by the glare of a car's headlights.

'I didn't say that!' Then, seeing her reaction to his outburst in her face, he clearly caught himself up and continued in what Liz felt was a voice which only the most ruthless control kept calm and reasonable, 'It's just that I feel that Nell and Mark sometimes miss out on the simpler things in life—like a walk in the rain, listening to music, or simply just sitting and talking by the fire.'

Liz suddenly had difficulty swallowing a mouthful of soup as her throat seemed to close up tightly. Richard's words had reminded her of the letters he had written to her; the man he had seemed to be in them. How had she lost touch with that man since she had actually met him in the flesh? Or had she lost him? Wasn't it just her own fears and the scars of the past that had made it seem so? 'Tell me about your marriage,' Richard had said, and perhaps in a letter she might have done so— but it was so very much more difficult face to face. Feeling suddenly restless, she got hurriedly to her feet, picking up the soup bowls and carrying them over to the sink.

'Do you ever wonder why Eleanor suggested that we wrote to each other?' she asked diffidently.

'Oh, that's quite simple—she thought I should make a new start.'

The crash of the spoons falling from her suddenly nerveless fingers into the soup bowls in the sink sounded unnaturally loud in the silence that followed Richard's words, and Liz found that her heart seemed to be beating high up in her throat, making it difficult to breathe naturally as she recalled the way Eleanor had pleaded with her to write to her brother, and the suspicion that had crossed her mind that perhaps her friend might be indulging in a some none too subtle matchmaking. But Eleanor had sworn that that was not the case—and, of course, she had never expected that Liz and Richard would ever actually meet.

'And have you—made a new start?'

'Not really.' Richard pushed back his chair and, getting to his feet, strolled over to where she stood. 'Like you, I'm still trying to come to terms with the way things went wrong last time.'

One hand came out, resting lightly under her chin, and turned her face gently towards his.

'You've gone quite white, Elizabeth. Is your head still troubling you?'

Numbly, Liz found herself nodding silent agreement, unable to admit that it had been the things he had said that had had this effect on her.

'Then why don't you go and sit down in the living-room? I'll make some coffee—unless you feel that that would make me some sort of domineering oaf.'

The hint of laughter in his eyes, the wry half-smile on his mouth, were irresistible, and Liz found her own lips curving in instinctive response.

'You may be domineering, but never an oaf.'

She saw Richard's eyebrows shoot up in an exaggerated display of surprise at the unexpected compliment and decided that the time had come to beat a hasty retreat. She didn't quite know what was happening to her; she found it impossible to keep up her hostility towards Richard, but the feeling of vulnerability and uncertainty she experiencd when she let her guard down was too much for her to cope with right now. She needed a few minutes' peace and quiet to gather her thoughts together.

'I—think I will go and sit down.'

She anticipated some satirical comment, something on the lines that she was running away from things that had to be faced, something she wouldn't be able to deny, but instead Richard simply nodded.

'You do that,' he said easily. 'I'll bring the coffee through when it's ready.'

She couldn't be *disappointed* by the ease with which he had let her go, Liz thought as she sat down on the soft cream cushions of the settee. She couldn't have wanted him to take things further, pick up her comment about his not being an oaf and turn it into something much more meaningful than she had intended, could she? It was impossible. But the feeling that coiled about her heart seemed to allow for no other possible explanation—and that told her that she had a lot of very serious thinking to do.

But there wasn't enough time for that. Far sooner than she had expected, and well before she was mentally ready, Richard was in the room with her, carrying two mugs of coffee, one of which he put down on the coffee-table beside her. Then, perhaps because, in spite of her struggle to hide it, something of her feelings showed on her face, her expression warning him not to come too close, instead of sitting down beside her as she had feared he wandered round the room, his own mug in his hand, studying the books on her shelves, the delicate watercolours on the walls, finally pausing beside her desk and lifting the cover of the typescript which lay on it, considering its contents with lazy curiosity.

'Is this the Balzac biography you're working on? It looks immense. How are you getting on with it?'

'I'm three quarters of the way through now.' Liz was grateful for the safety of the topic of conversation. 'Another couple of weeks should see it finished.'

'You got the job through Nell, I suppose?'

Liz nodded. 'Most of my work comes through Eleanor these days. In fact, it was her idea that I should work freelance in the first place.'

But it had been her own dream of long ago, a dream she had abandoned when she had married, believing that she would not be able to cope with starting up on her own and helping her husband to build up his own business.

'I wondered about that. After all, you already had a good, secure job. It must have been quite a risk, branching out on your own like that.'

Liz took a few moments to consider her response to that remark, taking care to think of the right way to phrase her answer.

'I didn't enjoy my job any more, but I couldn't afford not to work, so when Eleanor suggested that I did some translations for her it seemed the perfect answer.'

Which was the truth, but not all of it, and, far too astute for comfort, Richard went straight to the heart of the matter.

'What was wrong with what you were doing?'

'Oh—I'd got bored.'

Liz gave a private inner sigh of relief at the thought that her voice was as smooth and light as she could have wished, no unevenness betraying the way she really felt. She couldn't tell him of the torment she had felt at going into an office where everyone knew she was married and having to admit that she had left her husband. It had been impossible to bear the knowing glances, the sympathetic smiles, the careful changing of the subject when she came into the room, and worse than that was knowing that everyone was aware of how much she had adored her husband and so was speculating on just what had caused the break-up.

'I'd been doing the same thing for over two years and I wanted a change—so it all worked out very well for me.'

'You've never regretted making the move?' Richard's attention was still apparently on the typescript, but there had been a perceptible sharpening of his tone that worried her.

'Oh, no.' Ruthlessly she squashed down her feeling of unease, ignoring the other possible implications of his question. 'I love being my own boss. I can plan my hours to suit myself, take time off when I want. I don't have to go out to a noisy, smoky office——'

She sounded over-enthusiastic, she thought wryly, as if she was trying too hard to be convincing. And just who was she trying to convince? Richard—or herself?

Her account of the pleasures of being self-employed left out so many things—like the fact that those casually mentioned days off never actually occurred. For the past nine months she had buried herself in her work, taking on anything Eleanor could find for her to do. She hated not being busy, and so when she wasn't working she filled the time with cooking, cleaning, making soft furnishings for the flat.

'So life's pretty good these days?' The odd note in Richard's voice had intensified disturbingly.

'It's certainly hectic.' Liz's laugh was shaky. 'I have trouble fitting everything in.'

'Yet you found the time to answer my letters. Why, Liz?'

The question came with a deceptive mildness but the fact that he had called her Liz, the name he claimed to dislike so much, made Liz's heart lurch suddenly.

How could she answer his question when it was one she had been asking herself for months, never coming up with a satisfactory answer? But even as she hunted frantically for some sort of response Richard amended his question, altering its subject slightly.

'What exactly did Nell tell you about me?'

'She said you were—lonely.'

This time the unevenness would not be ironed out of her voice. Loneliness was a feeling that she knew only too well, but it was not an emotion that she easily associated with Richard Deacon, particularly not after yesterday, after seeing the suave, self-confident man who had met her outside the wine bar. Richard's snort of laughter made her glance at him sharply.

'Wasn't that the truth?'

'Depends how you define the term,' was the laconic response. 'Nell's going through a very maternal phase at the moment. I suspect that she wants another child though she won't admit it, so instead she's taken to mothering her baby brother, trying to put my life in order.'

'And you don't think that's necessary?'

Liz was having trouble trying to equate the picture of a lonely, desperate man who was in danger of going completely off the rails which Eleanor had given her with the composed, self-assured male who stood before her, the way his hands were pushed deep into his pockets the only possible sign of unease about him. He had discarded his jacket and tie and, in spite of herself, she couldn't help noticing the way the fine linen of his shirt clung to the contours of his chest and shoulders. He certainly didn't look like a man who had lost control of his life—for one thing, there wasn't an ounce of spare flesh on his lean, rangy body; in fact he was almost too thin.

'If it is, then I'd like to sort things out myself—and my way isn't necessarily my sister's. She may think that combining marriage and a career is the perfect blueprint for a happy life, but it doesn't work that way for everyone.'

Richard's dismissal of Eleanor's lifestyle was unexpected, and, as it was much the way of living that she had once tried to create for herself, his comment stung sharply.

'You value your success above everything else?'

The flash of fire in Richard's eyes, the suddenly savage look he shot her had Liz reeling back in her seat, feeling as if she had ventured too close to a firework that she had thought was dead, only to find it exploding in her face.

'Don't put words in my mouth!' Richard snarled. 'Right now, I don't know what I want. You should understand that—you——'

He cut off his words abruptly, drawing a deep, ragged breath, and with a sense of shock Liz saw the way his shoulders and arms had suddenly tensed, giving him the appearance of a man who was struggling to control some unbearable emotion.

'Elizabeth——' he said huskily, and the single word sent a sensation like the trickle of icy water down Liz's spine. She was suddenly very sure that she wasn't going to like the things he was about to say. 'I know you said that we should meet as strangers, but it isn't going to work. We can't pretend that we don't know that—certain things—have happened. We— '

'No!' Liz broke in sharply. 'I don't want to talk about it—any of it!' He was a stranger, and only as a stranger could she relate to him. If he tried to get any closer she would run in the opposite direction, as fast and as far as she could. 'I told you—I don't want to talk about my marriage!'

'*Your marriage!*' It was a violent explosion that made Liz shrink back in her seat, her eyes wide and dark with panic. '*Your* marriage! What about my part in all this? What about *our* marriage, Beth?'

CHAPTER FIVE

'WHAT about *our* marriage?'

Liz felt as if she were on a roundabout that was whirling out of control, threatening to send her spinning off into the air at any moment. Richard had broken all the rules, destroyed the careful, protective barriers she had built up, leaving her a prey to all the vulnerable feelings she had tried so hard to conceal, even from herself.

When Richard had first suggested a meeting, she had refused adamantly, rejecting the idea out of hand, knowing it would never work, that she could never cope with it. But he had persisted, slowly, insistently breaking down her resistance until she had realised that they couldn't go on as they were, that she couldn't continue their correspondence without actually seeing him. But she had known that to meet him as her ex-husband would be more than she could bear; she had felt that it would destroy her emotionally.

And so she had laid down certain conditions. She had agreed to the meeting only if they pretended that they were total strangers, two people who had never seen each other before; only that way could she face him without breaking down completely. And for a time the subterfuge had worked, for her at least. She had forced herself to think of him only as Richard, the man she knew through the letters he had written, and had put her husband out of her mind until now, when his angry words had stripped away the protective masks, revealing them as the façade they were, and forcing her to see him as Richard Lewis Deacon, the man to whom she had given her heart so completely, the man she had married, and whose lack of love for her had torn her world apart.

'Our marriage doesn't exist! It's over—dead!'

'And why?' Richard flung back savagely. 'Because you walked out on it without so much as an explanation!'

'Because *I*——' Liz choked on the word, unable to believe that *he* was actually accusing *her* of ending the marriage when anyone who wasn't completely blind could have seen what was happening. '*I* walked out! Our marriage was finished long before I left—there was nothing holding us together. You were never there!'

That point had hit home; it showed in the way his face changed, the angry light fading from his eyes, leaving them dull and flat as the sea on a calm grey autumn day.

'I wasn't at home as much as I'd have liked to be, I'll admit that, but—Beth, I——'

'I told you not to use that name!' Liz broke in, unable to bear the sound of the affectionate name she had heard so often in the gentle tones of love or the deep passion of their marriage bed—love and passion that she had believed in, that she had thought were inextricably linked, until she had been bitterly disillusioned.

'*Liz,*' Richard amended with bitter irony. 'So, tell me—why did you decide to become Liz Neal? Was Beth Deacon no longer good enough for you?'

Beth Deacon was all I ever wanted to be, but you destroyed my love for you! Liz had to bite down hard on her lower lip to hold back the agonised retort that almost escaped her. And now, as she had known would inevitably happen, the walls that had been holding back the truth from her mind while she tried to pretend that Richard was just a stranger, and which had been gradually crumbling like a dam which had been eroded by time until it was too weak to hold back the power of the water behind it, finally gave way, allowing memories to flood her mind in a raging torrent...

She had first met Richard Deacon at a very stuffy dinner party to which she had been taken by her current boyfriend during her last year at Durham University. Lionel wasn't a student himself, but an architect whom she had met in a local pub, and the dinner was being given by his boss, the senior partner in the firm.

Liz noticed Richard at once because he appeared as out of place in this elegant and largely middle-aged gathering as herself. Lionel was nine years older than she, and everyone else in the room a generation or more her senior, except for the slim, dark-haired man in the far corner who wore his smart suit with a faint air of unease that spoke of someone much more accustomed to casual clothes, and who was clearly making an effort to charm a large woman in an over-ornate emerald-green taffeta dress who Liz vaguely recognised as Marjorie Huntingdon, the senior partner's wife.

The charm seemed to be working, too, Liz acknowledged, seeing the colour that rose in the older woman's cheeks, the way she ducked her head in coy acknowledgement of what was clearly some outrageous compliment. That young man would go far, Liz told herself, and at that moment, as if feeling her eyes on him, he looked up and in a way that Liz recognised rather wryly as the oldest cliché in the book their eyes met across the crowded room.

But a second later she had forgotten her amusement as her gaze was caught and held and she was treated to a smile of such brilliance that it was like having a spotlight switched on right in her face. Instinctively she took a step backwards, planting her heel right on the toe of Lionel's shining handmade shoe, making him start violently, spilling some of his wine down his elegant suit.

'Oh, I'm so sorry!'

It wasn't just concern for his evident discomfort or embarrassment at the grimace of pain that made her so flustered and over-effusive in her apology. That smile had seemed to strike home with the force of a bolt of lightning, leaving her shaken and unable to think straight.

'No damage done——'

Lionel was clearly struggling to maintain his composure though it was obvious that he was annoyed at the way the incident had happened in front of his boss, and Liz knew intuitively that their short-lived relationship was over. He wasn't likely to suggest another date when he took her home tonight.

Not that she minded particularly; looking into his handsome, clean-cut face topped with smooth brown hair, she suddenly found that the attraction she had originally felt towards him had vanished as if it had been burned away in the blaze of that one amazing smile. Catching herself on the fanciful thought, she mentally shook her head in amazement. What was happening to her? She couldn't have been so affected by a single glimpse of a man she didn't know. She couldn't even properly recall what he looked like—all she could remember was that smile.

So when she found herself seated next to the dark-haired man at the dinner table, Liz studied him covertly from under her lashes. Seen close to, his wasn't exactly a conventionally good-looking face. Thin and finely sculptured, it was too narrow for real handsomeness, all hollows and sharp angles, with deep-set eyes under heavy brows and a long, straight nose which gave him a rather arrogant, almost autocratic look. The thickly waving dark hair was the only soft thing about him, more noticeably so because, when compared with the closely cropped styles of the other men at the table, it appeared rather long, brushing the top of his collar at the back of his neck.

Absorbed in her survey, she wasn't aware that the man had spoken, and started nervously when he repeated his question.

'Who are you? You're not someone's wife—I know I've met all of them.'

'I—no—I'm not married.'

Disturbed by the unexpected question and an inexplicable intensity in the sea-green eyes that now met her own, Liz lifted her left hand and waved it in an exaggerated gesture almost under his nose.

'I'm not even engaged.'

She could have sworn that a small smile of—what—pleasure? Satisfaction?—curved his lips just for a moment, but it vanished again before it had really registered on her mind.

'I thought not. You're far too young to be involved with anyone here.'

There was no mistaking the note of triumph in his voice now, and honesty forced her to add hastily, 'Actually, I came with Lionel.'

It was only when the light in his eyes faded that she realised it had been there and, listening to her own words again inside her head, she realised that they had been spoken rather over-emphatically, seeming to imply a relationship that didn't really exist.

'Ah, yes, Lionel,' he said cryptically, his gaze going to the top of the table where Lionel was deep in conversation with Mr Huntingdon, or, rather, listening to something his boss was saying, his intent expression implying a deep interest that Liz felt instinctively was carefully assumed in order to impress. 'Our Mr Edwards always did have an eye for a beautiful girl.'

Then, just as Liz was admitting to a warm glow of pleasure that the indirect compliment had brought, he turned back to her and with a quick, appraising glance took in her inexpensive dark blue dress, the chainstore jewellery at her throat and ears, and the inexpert attempt to put her hair up in a chignon which was already beginning to feel perilously insecure, and his expression altered subtly.

'But you're not at all his usual type.'

Liz's breath escaped in a faintly shocked gasp and, unable to stop herself, she blurted out, 'And just what *is* his type?'

His slow smile had none of the thousand-watt brilliance of the one he had given her earlier, but all the

same it had no less an effect, making her heart lurch
suddenly so that she was painfully aware of the hot
colour rising to her cheeks.

'Much more sleek and sophisticated. Our Lionel likes
his women to be decorative—something he can show off
to enhance his image.'

'And I'm not—decorative?'

It was a struggle to keep her voice low so that her
words weren't overheard by the woman on her right.
The warm glow had faded into something that felt uncomfortably like disappointment, making her tone high-
pitched and tart.

Blue-green eyes opened wide in a display of assumed
innocence so that she caught the gleam of amusement
in their depths and knew he was mocking her.

'Did I say that? You asked what type of woman Lionel
liked, and I told you. It must have been important to
you to know,' he added on a new note.

'Are you implying——?'

'I'm implying nothing—just answering your question.'

Liz was rapidly readjusting her original assessment of
this man. When she had first seen him she had compared him to herself, thinking that he looked as much
out of place as she felt, but now he showed no sign of
being ill at ease or uncertain; in fact his whole attitude
was that of a man who knew exactly where he stood.

'And don't fish for compliments. You of all people
should know that you don't have to do that.'

'Fish for——!' Liz spluttered indignantly. 'Look, I
don't know who you are——'

'Richard Deacon,' he supplied promptly. 'Very junior
member of the illustrious firm of Huntingdon and
Carr—for my sins.'

'You don't enjoy your work?' Liz couldn't hold back
her question, her curiosity aroused by his wry comment.

Richard's mouth twisted slightly. 'It's a start, but it's
not how I want to spend the rest of my life. Designing

supermarkets may be bread and butter money but I want
to do more than that.'

'What sort of things?'

'I want to create buildings that will not only be functional but beautiful—structures that blend in with their
surroundings and yet enhance them. There's too much
ugliness in the world already. A building is a work of
art just as much as a painting or a sculpture.'

That remark had ended their private conversation because it was overheard by Lionel, and in the discussion
that followed, becoming more general as everyone
around the table joined in, Liz found that she and
Richard Deacon were in a minority of two in their desire
to want to preserve the elegance of the past in the
buildings of the present. When it came to the techni-
calities she was well out of her depth, but at that point
Richard himself took over and she was able to sit back
and simply listen as he argued his case in clear, concise
terms, easily demolishing the reasoning of the others but
always remaining calm and courteous—in contrast to
Lionel who grew redder in the face and more aggressive
with each comment—and yet making it only too plain
that he thought their opinions foolish and narrow-
minded.

In the end, the debate was brought to a halt when
Marjorie Huntingdon spoke into a brief lull in the
conversation.

'Well, I think we'll continue our talk in comfort. If
you'd all like to go through into the lounge, coffee will
be served there.'

Her words were more of a command than a suggestion, and were accompanied by a glare in Richard's
direction that made him slant a wicked, glinting glance
at Liz's face.

'That's a black mark against me,' he murmured under
cover of the general bustle of people pushing back their
chairs and getting to their feet, the undercurrent of
laughter in his voice revealing how little that worried

him. 'Marjorie hates it if her dinner parties end up with us all talking shop, and I think she regards my ideas as subversive—little less than treason to her husband. Look——'

Richard caught hold of Liz's arm just as she was about to follow everyone else out of the dining-room, which was now empty except for the two of them.

'Do you really want to sit around and drink coffee for the rest of the evening?'

'Not really.' If Liz was honest, the idea didn't appeal at all. The truth was that until Richard had spoken to her she had been very bored indeed.

'Then let's get out of here. I'll make your apologies to Marjorie in the morning.'

Liz hardly recognised herself in the girl who, carefully suppressing an impulse to laugh out loud, grabbed her coat from the rack in the hall and followed Richard out into the cold, starry night, her mood suddenly very much like that of a child escaping from school on the last day of the summer term, with all the holiday ahead of her.

She wasn't usually this impulsive, rarely acting without thinking first, but she suddenly felt very light-hearted and vividly alive as never before. She didn't care what might happen; she only knew that she wanted to be with Richard, and the thought that he wanted to be with her sent her heart soaring, making the blood sing in her veins so that she didn't feel the cold wind that blasted her face as they crossed the pebbled forecourt to where Richard had parked his car.

'I'm afraid I don't aspire to Lionel's Porsche yet,' he said on a note of irony as he unlocked the passenger door of an elderly Escort and held it open.

'I never did like Porsches anyway,' Liz responded lightly. 'They're too flash to my way of thinking. This is much more comfortable.'

And, strangely, in spite of its well-worn interior, Richard's car *was* more comfortable. The seat seemed to enfold her body as if it had been made for her—it felt *right*—and when Richard slid in beside her she felt even more as if this was where she belonged, here, in this car, with this man at her side, her every nerve hypersensitive to the sight and feel of him so close to her, the warmth and scent of his body. Even his silence was comfortable so that she didn't feel any need to break it by launching into trivial conversation as she would have done with Lionel or other men she had dated. She felt happy to wait until he wanted to talk, happy just to be with him.

'I don't usually do this sort of thing,' Richard said after a time when they had left the Huntingdons' house behind and were heading for the road to Durham. 'I don't want you to think that I'm in the habit of kidnapping beautiful girls and absconding with them into the night.'

'So why tonight?' Liz asked, hugging that 'beautiful' to her like a warm, soft blanket.

In the light of a street lamp she saw Richard's brief, thoughtful frown.

'I don't know—it just seemed right.' Suddenly he laughed out loud, shaking his head as if in amazement at his own behaviour. 'Do you realise that I don't know anything about you except your surname? Charles called you Miss Neal.'

'Elizabeth Neal,' Liz confirmed. 'I'm a student at the university, studying languages.'

'Ah.' Richard made it a thoughtful, almost disappointed sound and suddenly Liz found that she was sitting tensely in her seat, the light-hearted mood draining from her like water from a bath when the plug was pulled out.

'Is that a problem?' she asked tautly.

'It depends,' Richard responded enigmatically.

It depends on what? Liz didn't ask the obvious question but waited for Richard to expand on his cryptic comment. But he added nothing further, instead lapsing into silence once more until they reached Durham where

Richard maneouvred the car to the side of the road and switched off the engine.

'Let's walk for a bit.'

He walked silently at Liz's side through the narrow streets, his long legs covering the ground swiftly so that she had to struggle to keep up with him. He appeared to be absorbed in his thoughts, and the frown on his face kept her from saying anything and intruding into his brooding abstraction. But when they came to the square before the cathedral she couldn't stop herself from coming to an abrupt halt, her hand going out instinctively to grasp Richard's arm.

'Look at that!' It was a gasp of awe and sheer delight.

Richard's eyes went to the tall, majestic building, its twin towers rising high into the sky, appearing eerily beautiful in the clear moonlight, and she knew by the change in his face that he was as affected by the magnificent spectacle as she was.

'It's wonderful, isn't it?' Liz's voice was low and slightly husky with the emotion of the moment and Richard's slight nod was all the encouragement she needed. 'Tell me about it!' she declared impulsively, adding as she saw his faintly puzzled frown, 'I can appreciate its beauty but I don't know anything about architecture—I can't see what you see in it. So, please, tell me about it!'

She wanted to learn, the need a deep inner yearning that she acknowledged came from a longing not just to know about the cathedral but also about the man with her, about the interest which absorbed him, which had driven him to make it his life's work. She wanted to get inside his mind, to know him, understand him better.

Later she was to recall with a sense of unreality that lecture on medieval architecture there in the deserted, moonlit square, Richard just a shadow at her side, his voice in her ear, opening new ideas, imparting new knowledge to her. She didn't know how long she stood there, had no idea whether hours or simply minutes had

passed, only coming back to herself with a strong sense
of regret when he finally stopped speaking and slanted
a wry glance in her direction, the moonlight catching his
eyes and making them gleam like a cat's.

'End of lecture,' he said drily. 'I'm sorry—you'll know
not to set me off next time.'

'I enjoyed it,' Liz assured him sincerely, struggling to
ignore the leap of her heart at that casual 'next time'.
'I feel as if I really know something about the place
now—and I feel rather ashamed that I've spent so much
time here without really finding out about it properly—
not understanding it, if you know what I mean.'

'I know exactly what you mean.'

Richard's voice had a new note in it, one that made
her breath catch in her throat and set her heart pounding
in a new and jerky rhythm. With an abrupt gesture she
dragged her eyes away from his, concentrating determinedly on the cathedral instead.

'It's awe-inspiring, isn't it?' She couldn't bring herself
to care that the shake in her voice revealed her words
for the careful cover-up they were. 'That new civic centre
Lionel so admires could never make me feel like this.'

'And it would never make me want to do this——'

Strong hands fastened on Liz's arms, turning her
gently but irresistibly towards him. She saw his dark head
lower and her heart seemed to stop for a second as instinctively she lifted her face towards his.

The touch of his lips was soft at first, strangely tentative as if he was unsure of her response, but then his
arms came round her, gathering her close against the
hard warmth of his body, and his mouth pressed hers
with a fierce determination. And all at once the sense
of rightness and completion came flooding back in a
glorious, glowing wave of delight.

This was where she belonged, this was where she
should be, and the beautiful setting, the glorious old
building, the moonlight shining down on them only
added to that feeling, making it seem as if she had wan-

dered into a dream world where everything was perfect, a wonderful delight, so that she responded to Richard's kiss with a willingness and enthusiasm that made him murmur her name on a note of stunned pleasure.

But then as Richard's exploring tongue gently probed her lips, easing them apart to deepen and prolong the kiss, Liz found that the wave of delight ebbed, to be replaced by a growing dissatisfaction that made her head reel as his hands slid under her coat to caress her body, the movement of his hands over the soft wool of her dress making the feeling grow, spiralling into a gnawing ache that made her want to cry out.

This was not enough. Every nerve in her body cried out for more than just these tantalising, unsatisfactory caresses, this closeness that wasn't complete. She knew then, intuitively and with total certainty, that the feeling of rightness she felt with this man would only be completely realised by the full intimacy of lovemaking, of knowing him as totally as it was possible to know any other human being. She wanted Richard, wanted him to make love to her, wanted it so desperately that her body strained against him, her hands clenching on his firm shoulders until every inch of her was pressed against his lean strength.

'Beth!' It was a groan of protest as Richard wrenched his mouth from hers, flinging his head up and drawing in deep, ragged breaths like a man who had come close to suffocation. 'Don't do this to me—not here—not now. I can't——'

Gently he disengaged her clinging hands, taking a step backwards, away from her, as his breathing slowed, became more regular.

'Beth, let me take you home——'

No one had ever called her Beth before, Liz reflected hazily. She liked the name much better than the 'Liz' her friends used, or her mother's strictly formal 'Elizabeth', and the husky intensity in Richard's voice, a lingering echo of the passion that had flared between them, sent a shiver of reaction feathering over every nerve so that she trembled visibly. If he took her home, he would want to make love to her—she knew that without any shadow of doubt—and that was what she wanted most in all the world, so she turned a glowing, vivid smile on Richard and linked her hand with his.

'We can walk—it isn't far.'

She felt as if she were floating on air as she walked the short distance to the house she shared with four other girls, and she was grateful for the fact that Richard had reverted to his earlier silent state so that she could simply enjoy being with him, hugging to herself the anticipation of what was to come. But at her door Richard stopped abruptly, making her turn a puzzled, questioning look on his strangely serious face.

'I'm not coming in,' he said, his voice sounding harsh and strained.

But she had been so *sure*. It had felt so right.

'You're not——' She couldn't complete the question. 'But *why*?'

'I have some thinking to do.'

Thinking? What was there to think about? Everything was perfect just as it was.

'I wasn't ready for this, Beth. It hasn't come at the right time. I don't intend to stay around here much longer—I want to move on, move up. There are so many things I want to do, so much I want to achieve. I already have an interview for a job lined up next week. If I get it, then with luck and a lot of hard work I'll be able to set up on my own in a couple of years. But if I take the job it means moving to Manchester.'

Manchester. The word echoed hollowly in Liz's head. He was moving on—and meeting her, the sense of rightness they had felt together, the flaring passion they had shared, would have no effect on his decision. His work was what mattered to him.

'So this is goodbye,' she murmured dully.

'Goodbye?' It came out on a harsh, questioning note. 'No, Beth, that's not what I mean—unless *you* want it to be like that. I just want you to know the facts—what my plans are. I know you'll have to stay here and finish your studies—until the summer at least—and I won't get much free time, I'll have to work almost every hour heaven sends. It won't be easy with you here and me in Manchester, but if you can handle that then I would like to see you again as often as we can manage it.'

'Well? What happened to Beth Deacon?'

'She doesn't exist any more. She was in the past—I've put her behind me.'

'And our marriage? Is that all in the past too?'

'What do you think?' Liz hid her private pain behind the tart retort. 'I decided it was time I learned from my mistakes.'

'That's all our marriage was—a *mistake*?'

'Why don't you stop this?' The few remaining remnants of Liz's self-control shattered completely. 'We didn't have a *marriage*—just a bolster to your ambition. Marriage is a partnership—sharing—each person giving to and taking from the other—but if one does all the giving——'

'Are you saying that was you?' Richard cut in on her in a low, savagely controlled voice that was more frightening than if he had shouted at her. 'I gave——'

'Oh, did you?' Seeing the way his face changed, knowing what he was going to say, Liz rushed on hastily. 'Oh, yes, you gave me *presents*!'

Bitterness laced her words with acid and she saw Richard's face whiten under the force of her attack.

'You gave me *things*—beautiful, expensive, meaningless gestures! They weren't what I wanted at all!'

'You——'

Richard got no further as the shrill sound of the telephone tore through his words and, grateful for any interruption, Liz snatched up the receiver with alacrity.

'Elizabeth?' Liz's heart sank at the sound of the familiar, crisp tones that carried clearly to where Richard stood.

'Your mother always had a wonderful sense of timing,' he murmured sardonically.

Instinctively Liz put her hand over the telephone mouthpiece, but too late—her mother had caught, if not his darkly ironical words, then at least the fact that they had been spoken in deep, masculine tones.

'Is there someone there with you?' Jane Neal questioned sharply.

With an effort Liz suppressed a sigh. 'Yes, Mother—a—friend.' She prayed that Richard's cynical snort of laughter didn't carry as his voice had.

'A *friend*?' Disbelief rang in her mother's voice. 'A *man* friend?' Taking her daughter's silence for acquiescence, she went on, still in that, to Liz's mind, appallingly clear, carrying tone. 'I should have thought you'd have learned by now that no *man* can be any sort of a friend. Surely your marriage proved that to you.'

'Mother——'

But Jane Neal ignored her attempt at protest. 'And that's why I'm ringing you. Enid Jameson told me that she had seen *that man* in town today.'

Automatically Liz's eyes flew to Richard's face as he stood beside her, clearly unashamedly listening to every word of the conversation, and her stomach clenched nervously as she saw the black fury that darkened his expression. They both knew only too well just who her mother meant by *'that man'*.

'I thought I ought to warn you that he was around. Lord knows what sort of trouble——'

'Mother!' Liz interjected desperately, trying to shut her mother up before she did any more damage. But it was already too late.

'That isn't who's there with you now, is it? Elizabeth, you know he——'

'*Mother!* I don't want to talk about him. He's no longer part of my life.'

Her voice shook painfully as a movement from the man at her side caught her eye and she saw how his hands had clenched into tight fists at his sides.

'That time is over. It should never have happened, I——'

The rest of her sentence was lost in a startled squawk as the receiver was wrenched from her hand and slammed down on its base with a bang that resounded through the flat. Grasping her shoulders roughly, Richard swung her round to face him and she quailed away from the savage fury that flamed in his eyes.

'So it's over, is it? It should never have happened?' he snarled viciously. 'Damn you, Beth, you talk about give and take, but you don't know the first thing about *giving*—not the tiniest little bit——'

He broke off suddenly, his eyes burning down into hers, suddenly deep and dark, his pupils so wide that Liz could see only the smallest rim of colour at their edge.

'Except in one way...' he went on, his voice rough and uneven in a way that sent a *frisson* of apprehension feathering over Liz's tightly strung nerves, her mouth drying as his dark gaze lingered on the soft outline of her lips so that unconsciously she wetted them nervously with her tongue. 'There was one thing you would give— and that's what I want to take now.'

'*No!*'

Liz's desperate gasp of protest and denial came too late and was smothered under the forceful pressure of Richard's lips, his kiss wild and savage, almost brutal in its determination. It was like no other kiss he had ever given her, not even in that final, devastating argument on the last night of their marriage, the night when she had decided that she must leave him. His mouth plundered hers roughly, forcing her lips apart, crushing them painfully as if he was determined to impose his domi-

nation on her. She struggled desperately to free herself
but his arms were like steel bands around her, im-
prisoning her against the solid wall of his chest so that
no matter how hard she twisted and turned she could
not get away.

She had to make her mind a blank, to blot out what
was happening to her body so that she wouldn't feel it,
wouldn't react in any way. But even as she struggled to
force her mind on to less threatening channels she knew
that her body was betraying her, that·it was already responding to the touch, scent and feel of the man who
had once been able to make her delirious with passion.
Like a finely tuned instrument that needed only the touch
of its master to draw out the magic of its sound, every
nerve, every cell was awakening, recalling those long-
denied pleasures and reacting instinctively to its needs,
ceasing to struggle, pressing closer to Richard, needing
to feel his body against hers.

As soon as Richard sensed her surrender his kiss lost
its fierce attacking quality and became gentle, teasing,
enticing, softly seductive, until a tiny moan of longing
escaped her. Knowing that he no longer needed to keep
her prisoner, he relaxed his confining hold, letting his
hands slide down the length of her body, a small laugh
of triumph sounding deep in his throat as, unable to
stop herself, Liz writhed in instinctive pleasure.

Her heart was pounding heavily, making her blood
throb in her veins as she felt the first feather-light caresses that tantalised and tormented, making the once
familiar aching longing uncoil deep inside her, growing
more and more intense with each second that passed until
it was a whirling spiral of desire that was close to pain.

'Richard!'

His name was a gasping cry, one that was choked off
as his hands eased the buttons of her blouse from their
fastenings and slid under the fine cotton to the silken
warmth of her skin beneath. For a few devastating
seconds more he tormented her with waiting, letting his

fingertips move in slow erotic circles just above the curve of her breasts until she murmured a husky wordless protest, need making her head swim, and only then, infinitely slowly, stretching out the sweet torment as long as possible, did he slide his hands lower, brushing over the white silk of her bra, his thumbs moving teasingly over her erect nipples, sending searing flashes of desire burning through her until finally he captured the soft weight of both breasts in his hands, his fingers closing over them possessively.

'Oh, yes, my lovely Beth.' Richard's voice was a harsh whisper in her ear, his breath warm against her skin, stirring the black strands of her loose hair. 'This is what you gave me—what I gave you. And it's the one thing that's still there. You can't deny it, Beth; you still want me as much as ever—don't you?'

His eyes blazed into hers, demanding an answer, and Liz knew he would see it in her face if she lied. But she couldn't lie; she was incapable of denying the truth. As she hesitated he moved his hands again, beginning those tormentingly exciting caresses once more.

'Don't you, my darling?'

It was that 'darling' that destroyed what little was left of her control, the memory of the times when he had whispered the word of love to her sweeping away all her defences.

'Yes!' It was a cry of despair, of longing and need. She was trembling all over and knew that her betraying reaction had not escaped him.'

'Yes.'

The single syllable, suddenly cold and curt, cut through the haze in Liz's mind like a razor-sharp sword and she swayed in shock as Richard snatched his hands away from her as if her skin burned him and stood regarding her coldly, no trace of the passionate lover of moments before lingering in the icy, set mask that was his face.

'Yes,' he repeated. 'I could take you now and you wouldn't resist. You talk about give and take, but you never knew how to give, Beth, not really, except in that one way, and really that wasn't giving but taking too— taking the pleasure I gave you and offering nothing in return. Well, it's too late, *Liz*. I don't want that any more—not without the rest of you. It means nothing that way!'

'It means nothing!' Liz spat the words at him as if they were acid in her mouth. 'How can you say that? You're the expert on meaning nothing!'

That brought him up short, a frown of confusion that she could almost have sworn was genuine clouding his face.

'What the hell are you talking about now?'

'You know what I'm talking about—you can't have forgotten—I certainly haven't—I could never forget the last night of our marriage—when you *raped* me!'

'*When I*——' Richard began but Liz couldn't bear to let him go on.

'But never again—do you hear? I want you to get out of here now—out of my life—and you are never, *ever* to touch me again.'

For one terrible moment she thought that Richard wasn't going to do as she said, that he was going to stay, possibly even to argue, and she knew that her dwindling emotional strength wouldn't hold out against anything he had to say. But then he swung round and snatched up his coat, not bothering to put it on as he strode towards the door. Her mind just one raw bruise of shock and pain, Liz followed him with her eyes, past knowing how she felt at seeing him go.

At the door Richard paused and turned back.

'By the way,' he said in a voice that stabbed straight to her heart with the deliberate and evidently false politeness of its tone, 'perhaps you could give your mother a message for me. Tell her that *"that man"* does have a name and I'd appreciate it if she'd use it in future.'

A grim travesty of a smile flashed over his face, making Liz quail inside.

'I wish I could say it's been good to see you, Elizabeth, but we both know that isn't true. You said you wanted me out of your life, so I'm going—I'll leave you to that over-valued independence of yours. But be careful—one day you might wake up and find that that's all you've got left.'

CHAPTER SIX

THE biography of Balzac was finished at last, and Liz posted off the manuscript with a sigh of relief. It had taken three weeks of solid, concentrated work, but now it was done and she was free.

Free to do what? Her mind threw the question at her, stopping her dead in her tracks. She had promised herself a holiday when this particular project was over, but now that that time had arrived she had no idea what she was going to do, and for the first time she faced the reality of the isolation of her life.

When she had left Richard, that isolation had been exactly what she had wanted. She had fled from their house in a moment of desperation, not really knowing where she was going. All her friends were Richard's too, and she didn't want to go anywhere where he might find her. Eleanor would have taken her in, of course, but, inevitably, her loyalties would have been split between her sister-in-law and her brother, and Liz was determined to spare her friend that. So instead she had followed the traditional path of all disillusioned brides and gone home to her mother.

And that had been a mistake. Jane Neal had never actually said, 'I told you so,' but the words had been implicit in every nod of her head, the way her lips had pursed tightly as Liz had poured out her story. 'I know, I know,' her expression had said. 'You don't have to tell me—I know all about the iniquities of men. Look at your father. He was unfaithful to me from the start—and then he walked out on me when you were only seven years old.'

After the first week, Liz had known that she couldn't stay with her mother, it would never work, and so she had found herself this flat. By then, of course, she had set herself up as a freelance translator, with Eleanor's help, and her work had kept her fully occupied. But working from home meant that she was forced to live a solitary existence. There was no chance to make new friends as she would have done in an office, and although that isolation had been something that she had actively sought in the first place, wanting the peace and quiet in which to lick her wounds and attempt to come to terms with what had happened, now it struck home to her with a force that left her shaken and disturbed.

What was wrong? Six months before, she had taken a couple of weeks off work and been perfectly content—in fact there hadn't been time to fit in everything she had wanted to do. But then she had only just moved into her flat and the cleaning, painting and decorating had been more than enough to occupy her—and, of course, that had been before Richard had come back into her life.

Richard. There was the reason for all her unsettled feelings. For the past three weeks she had managed to bury all thoughts of him under the pressure of the work timetable she had set herself, but with the book finished, and nothing else planned, she had too much time to think and she found herself brooding, going over and over the scene in her flat, hearing again the words he had flung at her.

'You talk about give and take, but you don't know the first thing about giving—not the tiniest little bit——'

How dared he accuse *her* of not giving? She had put everything she possessed into that marriage, making a home for them, entertaining Richard's clients—even going to that damned cookery course in order to be able to do the job properly. She had supported him totally in his efforts to build up his own business, and all the time she had been working at her own job too.

The sound of the telephone intruded into her thoughts and, grateful for the interruption, she reached for it swiftly.

'Hi!' Eleanor Baldwin's voice greeted her cheerily. 'I just wanted to let you know that the Balzac's arrived safely. You must have worked like a Trojan to get it finished so soon.'

'Oh, I——' Liz caught herself up hastily, realising that she had been about to say, 'I had nothing better to do.' It was the sort of remark that might just get back to Richard. 'I wanted it off my back so that I could take a couple of weeks' break.'

'I see—so now you're a lady of leisure——'

A small pause alerted Liz, making the tiny hairs on the back of her neck lift in apprehension so that she wasn't surprised by her friend's next remark.

'Have you heard from Richard lately?'

'I met him once—nearly a month ago.' She would have preferred not to admit to that, but Eleanor probably knew it already. 'It—didn't work out.'

'Yes, I heard about that. No details, of course—you know my brother, he keeps his thoughts very much to himself. I gather your mother put her size nines in it again.'

'She did rather,' Liz admitted ruefully, picturing Richard's darkly angry face when he had caught her mother's scornful 'that man'. What had he been about to say? What would he have said if her mother's ill-timed phone call hadn't interrupted him?

'And how is the old dragon these days?'

Liz couldn't help smiling at her sister-in-law's name for her mother. Eleanor and Jane Neal had never got on, and Liz had the suspicion that, illogically, her friend blamed her mother for the break-up of her brother's marriage.

'She's fine.'

'Still teaching at the tech college, and spending her evenings with the women's group?'

'And what's wrong with that?' Liz felt obliged to protest, disturbed by Eleanor's tone of voice. Surely as a career woman herself, she would be the first to defend Jane Neal's right to live her life the way she wanted.

'Oh, nothing—if that's the way she wants it. But I have to admit that it's always seemed rather sterile to me.'

'Sterile! Nell, don't be ridiculous! She has her work, her friends——'

'And love?' Eleanor put in sharply.

'You know how she feels about that. I've told you what happened.'

'Oh, sure.' Eleanor sounded distinctly sceptical. 'You told me what a bastard your father was—and the way she's let it ruin her life ever since.'

'No, that isn't true!' Liz flew to her mother's defence. She had always admired the way Jane Neal had rebuilt her life after her husband's desertion, bringing up her daughter single-handed, training for a career in teaching, finding herself a good job——

'Isn't it? Liz, love, lots of women are treated appallingly by their husbands, but they don't let it scar them permanently. There's nothing wrong with the way your mother lives her life, Liz. In many ways it's totally admirable, but she could have had so much *more*. She's so closed in on herself that she can't let love in, and that's what I find so very tragic.'

Eleanor's words echoed over and over in Liz's head long after the conversation had ended and she had put the receiver down. Scarred, embittered, sterile, empty, tragic—the terms Eleanor had used to describe her mother seemed to bombard her like tiny ice-cold pellets, making her head spin in shock because she had never looked at Jane Neal's life in quite that way before. Caught up in her admiration for the way that, at a time when Women's Liberation was not the fashionable concept it now was, her mother had made her own way in the world, she had never stopped to consider how much might be lacking in her life.

And now in her own, a tiny, unwelcome voice whispered inside her head, its effect like that of pressing a panic button so that her heart jolted violently, the blood draining away from her face, leaving it pale and ashen. Richard's words, 'I'll leave you to that over-valued independence of yours. But be careful—one day you might wake up and find that that's all you've got left,' sprang into her mind as clearly as if he had been standing in the room and had just spoken them.

'No!' she whispered, but even in her own ears the denial sounded false and uncertain as she faced the fact that Eleanor's comments mirrored the way she had been feeling about her own life lately, and that was something she had to think about.

She had been hurt, disillusioned, her marriage had failed, but was she going to live alone for the rest of her life, blocking out any sort of love as her mother had done? Ruthlessly she forced herself to face the prospect of a future with no one beside her, no warmth, no affection, no one to share things with, good or bad, no— she gave a choking cry—no children. At least her mother had had a child to care for.

Liz's mind swung away from the future and on to the past, reviewing the time she had spent with Richard. Their marriage had disintegrated painfully, but Richard himself, until that very last night, had never treated her badly.

Richard. It all came back to Richard. Before their meeting she had been quite content with her life—or had she? She had filled her time quite adequately, functioned as efficiently, day to day, as she had done before— but what about the long, long evenings with no one to talk to, and the endless empty nights?

And it had got so much worse recently. The truth was that she missed Richard's letters. Never before had she gone for so long without hearing from him, and that only served to bring home to her how much she had looked forward to his letters, how the days on which one had arrived had seemed somehow brighter, more vital.

She had treated him very badly, she admitted with a sigh. Their marriage was over but she could have handled things very much better. They could no longer live as husband and wife, but they should at least have been able to *talk*. And Richard had been so very kind and helpful when she had been ill and she had never even thanked him. She *should* have thanked him.

Coming to a sudden decision, Liz sat down at her desk and pulled out a writing pad and pen, wrote her address at the top of the page and began, 'Dear Richard'——

Then her mind went blank. It was strange; in the past she had found that the words flowed from her pen without her having to think, but after meeting him that easy communication had been destroyed. She could no longer think of him as some faceless stranger, a man she didn't know; he was her *husband*, the man she had loved so very much.

And *'Dear Richard'*—so many times she had written those words, using them only as a convention, meaning nothing, but suddenly they seemed to reverberate inside her head, sending echoes of significance out into her life like the ripples that flowed out from a stone thrown into a pond.

Would Richard even want to hear from her? Recalling the black anger on his face, that savage kiss, the bitter words he had flung at her before he left, she could well believe that he would never want anything to do with her ever again and she would do better not even to try to communicate with him. But her conscience wouldn't let her leave things as they were. She had to try to put things right, make some sort of peace with Richard before she could really put the past behind her and get on with her life. She couldn't leave things to fester, as she admitted they had done with her mother, turning the future as well as the past sour.

Pen and paper forgotten, Liz stared out of her window, seeing not her small garden, limp and damp on a dreary autumn day, but her mother's face the last time she had seen her, on the day Richard had called at her flat.

Alerted by the abrupt end to her phone call, Jane Neal had rushed round to her daughter's home, looking for all the world like a furious lioness determined to ward off an attack on her defenceless cub. She had been almost comically disappointed to discover that Richard had already gone, and, balked of the confrontation she had been anticipating, had rounded on Liz instead.

'What on earth were you thinking of, letting him force his way into your flat? You know what that man's like— the mess he's made of your life——'

'Mother!' Liz broke in protestingly. 'Richard didn't force his way in, I let him in.'

'You *let* him in! I suppose he just turned on the charm and you gave in—how could you be so weak, Elizabeth?'

'It wasn't like that. I was ill and he was—kind.' More than kind, her conscience reproached her.

'Kind!' Jane Neal repeated the word with bitter satire. '*Kind*—all men are kind when they think it will get them what they want. Donald Neal was *kind* to me each time I found out about his latest affair. He was very *kind* to me all the time he was seeing the eighteen-year-old he eventually ran off with, leaving me without any support whatsoever!'

Liz felt that she should be used to the way her mother's face changed whenever she spoke of her ex-husband, but somehow, this time, she found it intensely disturbing. She might not love Richard any more, couldn't live with him as his wife, but she didn't *hate* him as her mother did her father.

'You want to be careful, my girl, you're far too soft, and women can't afford to be soft or men will just trample all over them. For reasons of his own, Mr Richard Deacon might have been trying the gentle touch today, but that's because it suits *him*. He'll draw you in like a spider enticing a fly into its web, and when he's got you just where he wants you he'll use you. Men are only after one thing——'

'It wasn't like that!'

It *hadn't* been like that. Except at the very end, when he had been so appallingly angry, Richard had made no attempt to seduce her, and then, astonishingly, just when he had had her completely in his power, he had stopped with that final, cryptic comment. Both then and earlier when, in pain and under the influence of the tablets, she had been at a very low ebb, dangerously weak, so that if he had pushed just a little bit harder she would have given in, and he must have known it—he *hadn't* pushed.

'It's always like that! All men are the same, all tarred with the same selfish brush.'

She had heard those words so often, Liz reflected. They were so familiar to her that perhaps in a way she had switched off from them, but now, with Eleanor's words in her mind, she couldn't help reflecting on how much that narrow-minded way of thinking had cost her mother. She counted no man as her friend, she had refused to let love into her life, and Richard's reaction to her phone call showed that she had destroyed the sympathy and admiration her son-in-law had once felt for her.

Surfacing from her memories, Liz came back to the present with a small shiver and found to her consternation that her eyes stung with unshed tears. For a moment she stared blankly at the paper in front of her, not recognising what it was, seeing only the words 'Dear Richard', a terrible sense of loss tearing at her as she recalled how very dear Richard had been to her in the first few months of their relationship, in that wonderful new beginning when she had been so full of idealism and hope.

That 'see you again' had been a classic euphemism, as both of them had known deep down. The intensity of feeling that had been sparked off when Richard had kissed her in the shadow of the cathedral couldn't be held in check for very long. The physical distance between them, and the fact that she shared her flat with the other girls, had naturally imposed some restraints on them, but by the time Liz had visited Richard in Manchester at Christmas she had known that, inevitably, they would become lovers.

What she hadn't been prepared for was the sheer, overwhelming force of delight that physical union had brought her. After her mother's experience she had always been frankly sceptical of the claims made for the pleasure of sexual love. The information on 'the facts of life' that her mother had given her had been just that, facts, with no hint of emotional involvement. She had no idea that, because of the way she had been hurt, Jane Neal was determined to deny the force of her feelings for the man who had abandoned her, though, from the way Liz's blood burned at Richard's kisses and caresses, she had already begun to suspect that her mother had definitely understated the case. But even so she still wasn't ready for the tidal wave of passion that assailed her.

Liz shook herself hard, driving away the last clinging wisps of memory as if they were delicate cobwebs. The past was the past—over and done with. She had said so herself, and meant it. She had to put it all behind her and concentrate on the future.

So why was she writing to Richard at all? Because he *wasn't* behind her. She couldn't just shrug him off; he was something she had to deal with before she could think about any sort of future for herself. The memories of the wonderful times they had shared, the times before everything had started to go wrong, still lingered, and now they were mixed with the recollection of Richard's kindness, the gentle consideration he had shown when she had been ill. Such thoughts pricked at her conscience uncomfortably, telling her that, even if she would find it so much easier, emotionally, she could not leave things as they had been when he had stormed out. Just because they were no longer lovers, no longer man and wife if not actually divorced yet, didn't mean that they couldn't treat each other civilly. If anyone else—a friend—had helped her in that way then she would have been grateful; she *was* grateful, grateful enough to erase the bitter memories of the way his dark anger had led him to treat her—but she hadn't shown it. She had let him go without even thanking him, and that realisation shamed her into picking up her pen with a new resolution.

'We parted so badly after our last meeting, and, thinking back, I see that I never thanked you properly for the way you helped me. I really appreciated all you did, and I'd like a chance to tell you so to your face.'

She owed him that much; it would be cowardly simply to write it in a letter.

'Perhaps we could meet again for a meal, my treat this time...'

CHAPTER SEVEN

IF SHE was honest, Liz had to admit that when she had written that letter she had never actually expected Richard to answer it. After the way he had stormed out of her flat, the bitter, angry words he had flung at her, she had felt that he was never likely to want to see her again. But even so, and despite the fact that she had told herself that—and having salved her conscience with her offer of a meal—she had still found herself tensing at the sight of the postman, her heart leaping at the sound of something being pushed through the letterbox, only to sink again swiftly when she discovered nothing but the usual assortment of bills and junk mail on the doormat—and most of it for the other occupants of the house.

After six days which, even allowing for the vagaries of the postal system, was quite long enough for Richard to have received the letter, written a reply and sent it back, she had finally resigned herself to the fact that he was not going to respond to her olive-branch, something which she found unexpectedly difficult to accept, and so she had answered the ring at her doorbell that night without any trepidation or unease.

'You! What are you doing here?'

The eyes that met her startled gaze were as flat and calm as an inland lake, and Richard's voice held an equal lack of emotion when he answered her.

'You invited me for a meal.'

'But not like this! I—why didn't you let me know you were coming?' Even Liz herself couldn't tell if anger or apprehension, or a mixture of both, sharpened her voice.

'I didn't know myself until a couple of hours ago.'

Nothing showed in his face, making Liz wonder whether she was being over-sensitive or *had* there been a note in his voice that suggested that it had taken him a long time to make up his mind whether to come or not—and that he wasn't sure of his decision even now?

'I've been hellishly busy with the Roper contract—no time to call my own. I didn't know for sure if I could get away, and I rather suspected that if I gave you advance warning you'd have second thoughts and withdraw your invitation. Is it convenient now?' he added on a blatant afterthought. 'Or am I interrupting—anything?'

The slight, and probably deliberate, hesitation before the last word, the faint emphasis on that 'anything', made irritation spark in Liz's mind.

'As a matter of fact, I was just in the middle of a full-blown orgy with twenty different men,' she snapped sarcastically, using attack to disguise the fact that what really rankled was that casual 'I've been hellishly busy', the indifference of Richard's tone taking her straight back to the days of her marriage, reviving the feelings of resentment and disappointment she had felt then. But then sharp realism pointed out that she had no right to expect anything else. The time when she could have expected to come first in his life was long gone, she told herself, looking Richard straight in the face for the first time, and she immediately regretted her tart response.

Richard had lost weight and it didn't suit him. The finely carved face was etched too sharply, his brilliant eyes appearing almost too large above the thin, angular planes of his cheekbones. The soft, dark brown leather jacket hung loosely on his narrow frame and he looked tired, washed out, and disturbingly vulnerable, making her think worryingly of the way Eleanor had spoken of him. She had been afraid that her brother had lost control of his life, that he was working himself into the ground, not eating or sleeping properly. Seeing him now, Liz could believe that her sister-in-law's fears had not been as groundless as Richard had led her to suppose, and she was forced to reconsider her attitude and in spite of the turmoil in her mind managed an attempt at a smile.

'I'm sorry—obviously I didn't mean that. Won't you come in?'

Richard took a single step forward, hesitated, then stopped again, still on the far side of the door, his eyes, suddenly dark and searching, going to her face and studying it so intently that Liz felt that marks must be etched into her skin where his gaze had rested.

'There's something I wanted to ask you——'

He didn't add 'before I make up my mind', but something in his voice made Liz add the words privately in her mind.

'The last time I was here—that precious independence of yours—was it still there the next morning?'

Liz stared at him in confusion, unable to make sense of his question or his reasons for asking it.

'Of course it was. I've been coping perfectly.'

She wasn't sure she liked the choice of 'coping', it sounded too negative somehow, and a sudden rush of memory forced her to recall how strangely difficult she had found it to adjust, how lonely the flat had seemed for a couple of days after he had gone.

'I told you I'd be fine once the tablets took effect and I was,' she added hastily, suddenly afraid of what she had revealed, if only to herself. 'But, as I said in my letter, I really appreciated the help you gave me.'

Still Richard lingered, a tiny frown creasing the space between his dark brows as if even now he still wasn't sure what his next move would be.

'I think I will come in, thank you, Elizabeth.'

Elizabeth. The single word and the tone in which it was spoken told Liz exactly where she stood without any need for further explanations. They were back in the roles of strangers, once more behaving as the people who had written to one another for six months and who had met very briefly on that one night at the wine bar.

That fact should have made her relax, but, strangely, it had exactly the opposite effect, making her feel as if the ground beneath her feet had suddenly shifted, throwing her awkwardly off balance. She had been thinking of Richard as the man she had once loved, wanting, for the sake of those happy times they had shared, to make peace with him, but he had deliberately put her into the role of someone he didn't know, distancing himself from her as effectively as if he had moved to the other side of the world. Obviously those memories didn't mean as much to him as they did to her, she thought on a wrench of pain and disappointment.

'Of course, if tonight is inconvenient you've only got to say.'

The careful formality of Richard's tone tugged at Liz's already tightly stretched nerves until she felt that she was close to screaming. If he felt this way then she couldn't understand why he had come, except out of politeness. But then, of course, Richard's manners had always been impeccable, and one of the things she had always loved and admired about him was the fact that he was scrupulously fair, always ready to meet an apology halfway—just as he was doing now. The desire to match him with equal reasonableness drove her to answer him honestly.

'Not at all. I wasn't doing anything in particular, and I haven't eaten yet. A meal out would be a nice idea. If you'll just give me a few minutes to change...'

Her voice faded, dying in her throat as she saw the way his eyes surveyed her tall, slender body in the cream lacy sweater and woollen skirt, her stomach clenching nervously as they lifted to her face once more and she saw that they had darkened dramatically.

'You look fine to me.' Richard's voice was calm, smooth, still with that damnably formally polite note in it, totally at odds with the flare of desire in his eyes which all his rigid control could not disguise.

'But I've been wearing this all day and I'd—feel better if I freshened up. Help yourself to coffee if you want some while you wait.'

Dear lord, how could she have forgotten? In the sanctuary of her room Liz sank down on the bed and struggled to pull herself together. She had let herself forget how their last meeting had ended; forgotten that cold, deliberate assault on her senses, the kiss that hadn't been a kiss at all but a savage, premeditated attack, calculated to bring about the response he wanted.

And she had given him that response, she admitted despairingly. Hopelessly, foolishly weak, physically at least, where he was concerned, she had responded instinctively and so left herself open to the final, devastating insult of his rejection of her. She had taken that rejection to mean that he no longer cared for her in any way at all, that even the desire he had once felt for her was dead, but the look in his eyes just now had told a very different story.

What was it Richard had said? 'It's too late, *Liz*. I don't want that any more—not without the rest of you. It means nothing that way!' Could he really have meant that he needed some…emotion—her mind skittered away from the idea of love—rather than just sexual gratification? Was it possible that, after all, she had misjudged him?

No. She was thinking foolishly, letting sentiment cloud her judgement. What she should be remembering was the last night of her marriage, the night that had finally made her decide that she had to leave Richard, that he would destroy her if she stayed. He had made love to her that night—no, not *love*. He had taken her cruelly and selfishly, without a care for her feelings—but in spite of the way he had treated her she had been unable to stop herself from responding as she had always done. The attraction Richard Deacon held for her had always been lethal, powerfully overriding any sense of her own self-preservation.

The sound of the kettle coming to the boil in the kitchen and Richard moving to pick it up penetrated her thoughts, dragging her back to the present, and her situation now. She couldn't go through with this, she declared to herself, getting to her feet in a rush. She couldn't sit at a table opposite the man who had treated her so appallingly, make polite conversation, smile, pretend, as Richard seemed able to pretend, that he had never been any more to her than some sort of penfriend. The memory of the Richard she had first met, that softer, gentler man, had weakened her, burying the real truth about the person he had later become under an avalanche of self-delusion.

She had turned towards the door, meaning to march into the living-room, tell him to go, get out of her life, when another memory stopped her dead. Once more Richard's voice, harsh with anger, sounded inside her head. 'You talk about give and take, but you never knew how to give, Beth, not really.' Before her eyes floated a vivid picture of Richard himself as she had seen him just a few minutes before, making her recall once more the things Eleanor had said, the worrying reports that, because some residue of the feeling she had once had for Richard still remained in her heart, had finally pushed her into agreeing to accept that first, fateful letter.

With a sigh Liz turned back and headed for her wardrobe, yanking open the door to stare unseeingly at the array of clothes before her. Which was the real Richard? The man she had loved, or the man he had become? The confident, self-assured creature she had seen so often, or the lost and lonely man her sister-in-law had described? She didn't know, and there was only one way she could find out, and that was by going along with the idea of having a meal with him tonight. Perhaps they would talk and she would gain some insight into the enigma that was Richard Deacon—though she had to admit that she had no hope of actually enjoying herself.

*   *   *

And that was where Richard had surprised her. Because
from the moment she had returned to the living-room
it had seemed as if he had set out to make things easy
for her. The distance was still there, that carefully cool
politeness that had set her nerves so much on edge earlier,
but this time it was coupled with a charm and consideration that soothed her jangled feelings, made her relax,
start to talk—the conversation kept carefully to strictly
neutral topics—and finally begin to enjoy both herself
and Richard's pleasant, undemanding company.

That evening she had rediscovered so many of the
things that had attracted her to Richard in the first place:
his easy courtesy, his intelligent, interesting and often
witty conversation, the way he had of drawing people
out so that before they knew where they were they had
told him their life-story—always leaving them with the
feeling that his attention and interest had been focused
entirely on them and that never for a moment had he
been bored.

She had seen him like this so often in the past when
they had entertained prospective clients, and although
she knew that the final decisions had always been made
on the quality of his work, which was more than able
to speak for itself, it had also been clear that his overwhelming charm and easy manner had already predis-
posed the client in Richard's favour. But not for a very
long time had she had the full megawatt force of that
charm turned on herself, so that, after long months of
isolation and—yes, loneliness, she admitted to herself—
its potency went straight to her head like some powerful
spirits so that by the end of the evening she was in such
a state of intoxication that she felt time had flown by—
and it hadn't lasted long enough.

As a result, when Richard had suggested, with a casual
diffidence that went straight through the barriers she had
tried to erect around herself, that perhaps they could
meet again—see a play or a film—she had found herself

agreeing without pausing to consider whether such a move was wise or not.

And, surprisingly, she had never regretted her decision. In many ways it seemed as if Richard's visits now replaced his letters in her life, bringing the same pleasure, amusement and interest as they had done and, like the letters, never disturbing her or making her feel threatened in any way. It was as if they really were, as Richard was determined to pretend they were, two strangers who had just met, or perhaps two former friends who had lost touch for a long time and were now beginning to learn about each other once again.

So she was unprepared for the force of reaction that gripped her a couple of weeks later when, as they shared a drink in a village pub, Richard suddenly altered the subject of the conversation from the safe discussion of a film they had seen earlier that evening.

'I saw Nell the other night,' he said casually enough, but with an edge to his voice that had Liz suddenly tensing in her seat. 'She invited us both to dinner on Saturday.'

'Dinner——'

Liz knew her voice sounded unenthusiastic but she couldn't help it. She had visited her sister-in-law a couple of times since she and Richard had separated, but this was different. For one thing, Eleanor would assume that their presence at her table together meant that they were to be regarded as a couple once more, and that was something she wasn't ready to let anyone think when she didn't know how she felt about it herself. But there was another reason too, one that was too closely linked with past unhappiness for comfort.

'I don't think so——'

'Why not?' Richard's tone was worryingly sharp. 'You said you weren't doing anything this weekend.'

'I'm not, but——'

'But what? What is it, Elizabeth? Do you not want to be seen with me, is that it?'

'Oh, don't be ridiculous!' Liz responded rather too sharply as his words came close to what she *had* been thinking. 'We've been going out together for weeks now.'

'To the theatre, where it's dark—to a pub miles from anywhere—a *very* quiet restaurant . . .' Richard laced the words with dark irony. 'We never see anyone you know, anyone I know. Even Nell wasn't aware that we were—"going out together".' His mouth curled around the words in an expression of distaste. 'Does *anyone* know about us, Elizabeth?'

Liz knew exactly what the emphasis on 'anyone' meant; Richard might just as well have said, 'Does your mother know?' It wasn't that she was afraid of telling her mother, though it didn't take much thought to imagine how Jane Neal would react; it was more that she wanted to keep her time with Richard to herself, without the sort of outside pressures that had intruded before, at least until she knew just where she stood, something which was no clearer now than it had been on the day Richard had turned up at her flat in response to her dinner invitation.

'It isn't that simple!' Liz's head came up sharply, her gaze meeting fierce sea-coloured eyes that seemed to bore into her skull as if seeking to draw out her private thoughts.

'As I see it, it's perfectly simple,' Richard retorted coldly. 'I've already accepted Nell's invitation, so either we go together or I go alone. I want you there, Elizabeth. I want you to come with me.'

Liz's heart skipped a beat and she closed her eyes against the pain of a memory that she had tried to bury in the dark recesses of her mind. She felt as if she had entered a time-slip and was back in the time of her marriage, reliving once more that dreadful night just before Christmas when, mentally and physically exhausted by seasonal preparations and the pressures of the entertaining which had snowballed to gigantic proportions, she had arrived home late from work, thinking only of a snack meal, a hot bath and a very early night, to find Richard in the bedroom, obviously dressing to go out to yet another dinner party—one that she had completely forgotten about.

'You're late!' he had exclaimed reprovingly. 'You'd better get a move on. If you hurry we can just make it.'

Liz froze in the doorway, staring at his face reflected in the mirror, seeing the impatience and annoyance stamped on it in hard lines. Once, she had accurately remembered every single dinner, every appointment with a potential or established client, remembered and planned her own preparations down to the last detail, determined to make Richard proud of her. But that had been in the days when such dinners had been few and far between; now it seemed that they were entertaining or being entertained almost every night of the week and she was sick of it. And Richard had long ago ceased to even hint that he was proud of her. In the early days of their marriage he had always found time to comment on her appearance, the food, the décor—now it seemed he just took it all for granted and the harder she worked the less he appeared to notice.

For a while now she had known that they were drifting apart; just recently they had been living almost separate lives, and she could no longer convince herself that the problems were only temporary, brought on by Richard's necessary concentration on the work that, from the beginning, he had made plain was so very important to him. He had his own firm now, it was securely established and doing well, but still Richard showed no sign of easing off the pressure—if anything, his single-mindedness was becoming worse. Her mouth set in a stubborn line. She was worn out and the last thing she wanted to do was to attend yet another dinner party.

'I don't want to go,' she declared mutinously.

It was the wrong thing to say, she knew that as soon as she saw his face change, his jaw tightening and drawing his mouth into a thin, hard line.

'And I want you to come with me,' he returned, his voice cold. 'I want you to be there.'

Something snapped inside Liz's mind and she rounded on him swiftly.

'Well, I'm not going! If this evening is so damn important to you, you can go on your own!'

Liz stirred restlessly in her seat as she remembered the ensuing explosion, the dark anger that had burst out of Richard in a flood of savage, cutting remarks until she had walked out of the room, locking herself in the spare bedroom and refusing to come out. She hadn't had to stay there long. A very short time later, the slamming of the front door and roar of a car's engine announced the fact that Richard had taken her at her word and had gone on his own.

He hadn't come back until early the next morning, by which time Liz, who had foolishly expected that as soon as he had calmed down he would make some excuse to the Henshaws and leave early, hurrying back to her to apologise, had grown tired of waiting for him. Sitting alone in the house, she had brooded over her wrongs, going over and over the scene and others so like it, her anger growing with every second that passed, so that when she finally went to bed she had left Richard's clothes in a neat pile on the landing and had locked the bedroom door firmly against him.

And now it was happening all over again. Once more, Richard had made it painfully clear that what *he* wanted was what mattered; the question was, what was she going to do about it? Richard's ultimatum left her in no doubt that if she refused to accompany him to Eleanor's he would go on his own. She would be left on her own as she had been that Christmas—but this time, would Richard come back? The repercussions of her refusal a year ago had left her with savage mental wounds from which she was still struggling to recover, the events that had followed that night still too painful even to contemplate, and she had no desire to expose herself to anything like that ever again.

But why was Richard so insistent that she go with him? Eleanor was his sister, not some prospective client who needed to be wined and dined and entertained by a charming hostess.

'I know how busy Eleanor is,' she protested inadequately. 'I wouldn't want to put her to any trouble.'

'It'll be no trouble.' Richard dismissed her clumsy excuse with a wave of his hand. 'Nell will have everything organised.'

Eleanor always had everything superbly organised, and that was part of the problem, Liz reflected on Saturday night as Richard's car drew up outside his sister's home. Eleanor was organisation personified, her home, her family, her job all running like some finely tuned machine. In a way it would have been easier if she hadn't actually *liked* her sister-in-law quite so much, if she could have found her, as she found Richard's mother, a rather cold and distant person, someone it was difficult to get to know. But Eleanor was always warm and open, a friend as well as a sister-in-law, which made the feelings of inadequacy and uncertainty she inspired in Liz so much more difficult to deal with.

Both Eleanor and Eve Deacon were that modern phenomenon, the superwoman, and Liz could still recall vividly her first visit to Richard's mother's immaculate home. As a homemaker, cook or hostess her skills were unsurpassable. Her house was a haven of comfort and elegance, her guests' every need was catered for, and every morsel of food was home-cooked from fresh ingredients, the most complicated of meals seeming as simple to her as something like beans on toast would be to Liz herself. She also had an incredible knack for choosing the perfect present, taking a lot of time and trouble in wrapping and decorating even the parcel so that it always appeared like a work of art—something

Richard had inherited from her, memory added with a twist of bitterness.

Liz could feel those old, remembered feelings of inadequacy reach out to enclose her once more as Mark Baldwin ushered them into the immaculate living-room, an open door at the far end of it offering a revealing glimpse of a highly polished table laid with shining silver and sparkling crystal, a glorious red and white flower arrangement forming a perfect centre-piece that exactly toned with the dining-room's décor. They were early because Richard had wanted to see Rachel, his niece, before she went to bed, but Eleanor, of course, was ready for them, superbly dressed as ever in midnight-blue velvet, her thick dark hair fastened in a complicated braid at the back of her head, and looking supremely relaxed as she rose from the settee to greet her guests with a welcoming smile.

Liz found her own smile in response was weak, her composure severely threatened as she was unable to stop herself from comparing her hostess's easy manner with her own harassed feelings whenever she and Richard had given a dinner party in the past.

The sort of formal entertaining Eleanor Baldwin and her mother seemed to manage so easily had been totally new and unknown to Liz before she had married Richard. It was all a far cry from the hastily snatched meals her mother had provided in between one project and another or the casual, plates-on-knees get-togethers of her university days, and she had had little time to adjust before just that sort of entertaining became central to Richard's life. When Richard's career had taken off, far sooner than either of them expected because the senior partner in his new job was much more sympathetic to his ideas than Charles Huntingdon had ever been, she had worked hard to become the sort of wife who would be an asset to him. As time went on, she had got better at it, but she had never been able to relax and was always rushing around at the last minute, making final preparations, barely having time to wash and change herself, never managing to achieve the perfection Eleanor created so effortlessly. But, in the beginning, all the effort and stress had been worth it, because Richard had seemed so proud of her. It was later, when he had become critical, even hostile, that things had started to go wrong, and from then on it seemed that the harder she tried the more difficult things became.

'It's wonderful to have you both here together again.' Eleanor's genuine enthusiasm took away the private sting of that 'together' but the single word made Liz pause to consider a new idea.

She had visited Eleanor and Mark several times since she and Richard had split up, and although she had been impressed, as always, by the way Eleanor ran her life, it was only now, *with Richard*, that those old feelings of inadequacy had gripped her.

'Mark, love, will you get Liz and Richard a drink?'

And that was another thing that stabbed sharply in Liz's over-sensitised mind. The warmth in Eleanor's voice when she addressed her husband, Mark's smiling response, were in stark contrast to the way she and Richard had often been at the beginning of a dinner party when Liz's tension and exhaustion had boiled over into a full-scale row which had had to be swiftly covered up with a hasty switch to stiff politeness when their guests had arrived.

'Liz, I must tell you, the publishers were delighted with the Balzac. I can get you all the work you want from them in the future.'

'That's wonderful!!'

Liz's natural delight was enhanced by a warm glow of appreciation for the way Eleanor had, unknowingly, offered her a lifeline of self-esteem. Her work at least was something she could do well, something to be justifiably proud of, and she felt her confidence blossom strongly.

'Tell them I'd be glad to work on anything——'

'I thought you were taking a holiday,' Richard cut in sharply. 'You said you wanted to go away——'

'Oh, that can wait,' Liz returned swiftly, disconcerted by his unexpected response. The truth was that she had forgotten that she had told him that she planned to take a holiday, and at the time she had said it only to keep the conversation going. And anyway, who was *Richard* to imply criticism of someone working too hard? 'This is important. I would have thought you'd understand that. My job matters to me, I have a reputation to build up, and to do that I need commissions——'

Her voice faltered as she saw the way Richard was looking at her, his eyes suddenly dark and probing. Was he, like her, remembering the number of times he had said those words or something very similar when she had complained that *he* was always working?

For long, taut moments their eyes locked together and Liz found herself tensing, waiting for Richard's response. But then, surprisingly, he simply shrugged dismissively.

'You *have* changed,' he murmured in a tone that made it impossible for Liz to decide whether his words had been a compliment or a criticism before he turned away to continue his conversation with Mark.

The meal Eleanor served them was everything Liz would have expected it to be, every course perfection, every mouthful delicious, and at the end Liz leaned back in her chair with an appreciative sigh.

'Nell, that was marvellous! You've really excelled yourself this time. You must give me the recipe for that salmon mousse.'

At the opposite end of the table Mark glanced up suddenly, his gaze going to his wife, the look that they shared somehow secretive, almost conspiratorial, and touched with a hint of amusement as Eleanor laughingly brushed aside the compliment.

'I'm just glad you enjoyed it. You know I like entertaining——'

'*Like* entertaining!' Mark's amusement was more pronounced now. 'You love it—and like your mother you make an art of it. Everything has to be done with STYLE.' His tone put the last word into capital letters. 'Now *I'd* be quite happy with a couple of pints and a take-away.'

'Men!' Eleanor rolled her eyes in exaggerated disgust. 'They're all the same, aren't they, Liz? Basic in the extreme.'

Liz could only manage an inarticulate murmur that might have been agreement, her thoughts going to the moment earlier in the evening when she had realised that her feelings of inadequacy only assailed her when Richard was with her. From that first visit to Eve Deacon's house, she had always assumed that that style was what Richard was accustomed to, that, like Eleanor, it was what he wanted in his own life, but Eleanor's words had seemed to include her brother as well as Mark in her laughing condemnation.

At that moment Richard glanced up suddenly and, meeting his dark eyes across the candle-lit table, Liz found that her hand was disturbingly unsteady so that she had to set down her coffee-cup with a betraying clatter as it hit the saucer. In the back of her mind she could hear Richard's voice saying, 'It's just that I feel that Nell and Mark sometimes miss out on the simpler things in life,' and her heart started to race uncomfortably as she was forced to reconsider those long-ago assumptions.

Had those dinner parties been what Richard had wanted, or had they been imposed on him by the demands of his job? In the beginning they too had found time for 'the simpler things'; it was only later that they had become trapped in the endless round of entertaining.

Trapped. The word reverberated round and round in her head. That was how *she* had felt, but she had assumed that Richard had enjoyed the formal dinners—certainly he had seemed very much at ease, at his charming best, during them. But the younger Richard, the man she had first met, wouldn't he, like Mark, have been quite content with a pint and a take-away?

'Talking of Ma,' Eleanor said now, referring to Mark's earlier comment, 'I saw her yesterday. Would you believe that she's finished all her Christmas shopping—and wrapped it?'

'And no doubt there's been a cake and a pudding maturing in the larder since summer,' Richard put in drily, 'not to mention six dozen mince pies in the freezer.'

'What's wrong with that?' Liz knew her voice sounded too tart but the mention of Christmas had made her nerves clench in nervous response. 'It makes life so much simpler if you're prepared well in advance. There's so much to do at Christmas——'

'Whatever happened to spontaneity?' Richard cut in, a harsh edge to his voice making Liz stiffen in her seat.

'That's fine if you have time for it!' she flashed back. 'But when it all has to be done, and you've a job as well——'

It wasn't just the reflection of the candle flame that had flared in his eyes, she realised, catching in her breath sharply. It was a blazing response to her outburst leaving her in no doubt that, like her, he too was remembering that last dreadful Christmas. Well, she hadn't told him then just why she had been so resentful—but she would damn well tell him now!

'And when no one else is prepared to help you do any of it,' she continued furiously, grey eyes flashing defiance at him. 'Then you have to work damned hard to get it all done, and a little early preparation makes life easier.'

Richard hadn't always left her to do everything, honesty forced her to admit to herself. At the start he had been willing to share the household tasks when the demands of his job left him free to do so, but that first flush of enthusiasm had very soon faded and he had opted out completely, leaving her to manage as well as she could on her own.

'That's your mother talking,' Richard returned icily. 'I can hear her voice in every word you speak.'

'And what's wrong with that? My mother was left with nothing, but she pulled herself up from rock-bottom—*by herself*. Everything she has, she's earned for herself.'

'I know.'

'And perhaps the most important thing she taught me,' Liz rushed on, ignoring Richard's quiet interjection, 'was that I had to rely on myself if I wanted to get things done. That was the way she lived her life——'

'We all know that your mother is a very determined woman.'

Liz didn't like the way Richard had phrased his comment, or the intonation he had given it.

'I know you never really liked her!'

'You're wrong, Elizabeth,' Richard responded with icy calm. 'Or, rather, you've got it the wrong way round. I could have liked your mother if she'd let me. I've always admired and respected her and felt that she deserved much better than the treatment she got from your father, but she never let me—or any man—get near her.'

'Which is hardly surprising! Mother doesn't need anyone—she lives a full, busy life——' The memory of her mother's face the last time she had seen her, the bitterness that had spilled out when talking about her husband, made doubt slash through her forceful assertion, making her voice hold rather less conviction as she continued, 'Her belief in women's capabilities are deeply important to her. They're what kept her going when——'

'I'm not denying that! It's the effect that belief has had on you that disturbs me.'

The effect on *her*? Completely taken aback, Liz couldn't think of any way to respond, and after a noticeable pause the sudden awkward silence was broken by a tactful cough from their hostess.

'More coffee, anyone?' Eleanor asked, the over-careful airiness of her tone bringing Liz back to the present with a rush and making her aware of the way she and Richard had ignored Eleanor's and Mark's presence, their attention centred on each other, intent on getting their personal points home. Only now did she realise how they faced each other across the table, both leaning forward, hands resting on its polished surface, so close that if it hadn't been for the floral centre-piece they would actually have been touching, their positions physically excluding their hosts as their confrontation had done emotionally.

'No, thanks, Nell.' Richard was the first to recover his composure. 'As a matter of fact, I'm afraid we'll have to be going. I know it's early,' he went on, firmly forestalling the protest that Liz had been about to make, 'but I do have to drive back to Manchester tonight.'

His attention was directed at his sister, only the tiniest flash of a glance revealing that he even remembered Liz was still there, but there was a tightness about his mouth, echoed in his over-precise movements as he stood up and carefully replaced his chair, that spoke of strong emotion held ruthlessly in check for the sake of politeness.

He hadn't finished with her yet, Liz thought on a shiver of apprehension as, knowing there was nothing else she could do, she followed his lead and made her way into the hall to collect her coat. He meant to continue with this argument—probably as soon as they were out of the house.

Partly to delay that moment, but also because courtesy demanded it, Liz paused in the hallway and took Eleanor's hands.

'I'm sorry about that,' she said, still embarrassed by the way she and Richard had launched into their own private battle over the dinner table. 'I don't know what happened——'

'Forget it! It made a change from a discussion on the latest contract or the architectural atrocities committed by some town planners. Besides——' her grip on Liz's hands tightened briefly '—it was good to see you two talking properly for once.'

Talking! Liz wanted to exclaim, but at that moment Richard joined them, kissed his sister and, with a firm pressure of his hand against the small of Liz's back, guided her irresistibly towards the door. They hadn't been *talking*. Richard had been trying to impose his opinions on her and he hadn't liked it one little bit when she had contradicted him.

And now the second part of the argument was bound to come. Determined not to let Richard get the upper hand, Liz waited only until they were in the car and turning the corner at the end of the road before she rounded on him.

'And just what did you mean by all that?'

Characteristically, Richard did not bother to pretend that he didn't know what she meant.

'Your mother is a very strong personality, Elizabeth, she has very definite views on life—the reasons for which we both know, but that's *her* life, not yours.'

'I know that!' Suddenly and irrationally Liz hated the way Richard said 'Elizabeth'; it sounded so cold and hard, totally without feeling.

'Do you? I wonder if you really do? You're twenty-six—how long are you going to let your mother run your life?'

'My mother—she *doesn't*!'

The denial sounded harsh and over-loud in the confined space of the car, Liz's private pain making the words come out much more forcefully than she had ever intended. It hadn't been her mother's views that had ruled her life. If anything could have been said to have done that it was the love she had once had for Richard, a love so strong that she had been prepared to give him anything he asked, until one day she had realised that she was the only one doing any giving and that had broken her heart. Yes, she supposed she was like her mother in that.

'Prove it.'

The two words sliced through the darkness like a sword and abruptly Richard slowed the car and guided it to a halt at the kerb, turning towards her, his face just one dark shadow outlined against the night sky by the light of a street lamp opposite.

'Prove it to me, Elizabeth,' he went on, and because she couldn't see his expression she felt his words like blows on her suddenly tightly stretched nerves as she saw the way the conversation was heading. 'Stop pussy-footing around and show me that you're your own woman and not just your mother's clone.'

'I don't know what you mean!'

But deep inside she *did* know—knew that, on this matter at least, Richard was right, she had been letting her mother rule her life. She could explain away the fact that she hadn't told her mother she was seeing Richard by claiming that she wanted to wait until she knew exactly where she stood in her own mind—and, after all, she had never anticipated that things would go on this long—but the truth was that she knew exactly what her mother's reaction would be. It would be like the time she had said that she was getting married—only much worse.

'I want to talk to your mother, Elizabeth.'

'No!' Liz's stomach coiled into tight, protesting knots at the thought of a confrontation between Jane Neal and the son-in-law she still referred to as 'that man'.

'*Yes!*' Richard declared adamantly. 'And the sooner the better—tomorrow would be best. I intend to see your mother, Elizabeth—the only decision you have to make is whether I go alone or with you.'

Liz closed her eyes in something close to despair, knowing that the only thing that would be worse than facing her mother with Richard there would be the thought that they had met and she had no idea what had been said.

'We'll go together,' she said, her nerves clenching in sudden panic as she realised the intimacy implied by those three words.

CHAPTER EIGHT

'MOTHER, this is ridiculous!'

After only half an hour Liz had had enough. Her mother hadn't, as she had feared, been openly aggressive or rude, though there had been a moment when she had first opened the door to them and, seeing Richard, had looked as if she was about to slam it right in his face. Instead, she had been impeccably, coldly polite, the only indication of her frame of mind the way she had blocked anything Richard had said, turning to her daughter instead and answering as if he weren't there. Richard had been amazingly tolerant so far, but, knowing the signs—the darkening of his eyes, the tight muscles around his jaw, the clipped edge to his voice— only too well, Liz knew that he was perilously close to losing his temper and so she hurriedly suggested coffee as an excuse to get her mother on her own in the kitchen for a moment.

'I don't know what you're talking about!' Jane Neal spooned coffee into the filter machine with abrupt, jerky movements that made a nonsense of her coldly calm voice.

'Oh, don't give me that!' Liz exploded in exasperation. 'You're behaving as if Richard were the Thing from the Pit—and all he's done is try to talk——'

'It's that *talking* I'm worried about! You know how I feel, Elizabeth. All the charm in the world doesn't impress me. As Shakespeare says, "one may smile, and smile, and be a villain"—and they usually are. Wasn't it bad enough that he ruined your life once without your giving him the opportunity to do it all over again? I thought you'd learned from your mistakes.'

Which mistakes? The question sprang unexpectedly into Liz's mind. The mistake her mother meant was letting Richard into her life at all, putting her trust in him, giving him her love. But had there been other mistakes, ones that she was only just beginning to realise that she might have made?

'I'm trying to,' was all she could manage.

'Then you should try harder! You know as well as I do that that man will——'

Jane Neal broke off abruptly, her eyes suddenly wide as she looked towards the kitchen door behind Liz's back. A cold hand seeming to grasp and twist every nerve in her body, Liz turned slowly, knowing with a sense of dreadful inevitability what she would see.

Richard lounged in the doorway, his apparently indolent pose belied by the white marks of anger around his nose and mouth and the way his eyes, dark and icy as an arctic sea, were fixed on her mother's face.

'That man will...?' he prompted harshly, his tone sending shivers of apprehension down Liz's spine. 'Tell me, Mrs Neal, what *will* that man——' he gave the words a savage twist of black irony '—do to your daughter?'

It took Jane Neal perhaps ten seconds to recover her composure but in that time Liz felt as if her racing heart had moved from her chest up into her throat, so that she found it difficult to breathe naturally.

'Do you have to ask? Haven't you done it already?'

'I'd like to know precisely what you think I've done.'

'You took my daughter's trust, her future——'

Not her love, Liz noted. Her mother would no longer admit that such an emotion existed.

'You ruined her career——'

Oh, Mother—*no*! The words formed on Liz's lips but she couldn't speak them, Richard's reaction freezing her tongue in her mouth. Abandoning its indolent position, his whole body suddenly snapped upright, his eyes narrowing swiftly as he shot a searching glance at Liz's stricken face. How could you? she thought despairingly. How could you tell him that?

'Correct me if I'm wrong——' the silky menace in Richard's voice betrayed nothing of the shock he must have felt which had been revealed in his sudden movement '—but my recollection is that Elizabeth had a job——'

'A *job*.' Jane Neal emphasised the word contemptuously. 'Working in an office. What about her dreams—her ambition to go freelance?'

'Mother!' Liz groaned as once more the force of those probing sea-green eyes was turned in her direction, transfixing her like a rabbit caught in the glare of a car's headlights. For a long, taut moment Richard simply stared at her, and when he finally spoke there was a disturbing edge to his voice.

'I knew nothing about this.'

'It was just an idea I had,' Liz tried shakenly, but Jane Neal wasn't going to leave things there.

'You didn't care to know!'

With a rush of relief Liz saw Richard's eyes move back to her mother's face, though she doubted that he had actually believed her clumsy explanation. She could expect some very close questioning on that matter before Richard would let it drop, she knew, and the prospect was not at all appealing.

'You're like all men.' Liz's mother was well into her stride now. 'Totally selfish, thinking only of what *you* want——'

'*All men?*'

For the first time Richard's voice rose above the rigidly controlled level in which he had conducted the whole conversation, then suddenly he seemed to pull himself up.

'I'd like to show you something, Mrs Neal,' he said and the change in his tone, its sudden gentleness after the bite of anger of a moment before silenced even his opponent as he moved forward into the room, pulling several photographs from his pocket as he did so. 'I'd like you to look at these——' keeping two photographs separate, he held the other two out to Mrs Neal '—and tell me who they are.'

The incomprehension on Liz's mother's face deepened as she glanced impatiently at the two pictures.

'Myself——' she indicated one with a wave of her hand '—and Elizabeth. But what——?'

'And these, Mrs Neal,' Richard persisted, still in that quiet but insistent voice. He placed the two other pictures over the first ones. 'What about these?'

'Well, obviously that's you and . . .'

The way her mother's voice faded away, her sudden pallor, alerted Liz and she moved to her side to discover just what had disturbed her so much. What she saw made her catch her breath in shock and she turned dark, puzzled eyes on Richard's face. How had he come by a photograph of her father?

A moment later she recalled that the picture, hidden away years before when she was seven, when her father had left home for good and her mother had destroyed every photograph of him in existence, must have been left behind among the things that she hadn't taken with her when she had left Richard.

'Who is that, Mrs Neal?'

'Don——' Jane Neal managed at last, in a strangled voice. 'My husband.'

As she spoke, her face changed, and, seeing the pain that darkened her eyes, Liz realised on a rush of intense sympathy that, in spite of all her declarations to the contrary, her mother had never stopped loving her husband. She longed to go to her, take her in her arms, but knew instinctively that Jane would reject any such gesture, particularly in front of Richard. And even if her mother would have let her, she doubted that she could have moved if she'd tried. Richard's tone, his grave expression, held her mesmerised, and she could only wait in silence to see what he would do next, what all this was leading up to.

'So——' Richard dropped the photographs on to the kitchen table and moved them round in a circle with light touches of his long hands. 'Jane—Elizabeth——' His fingertips brushed each picture as he spoke. 'Richard—Donald——'

Suddenly he glanced up, his dark, intent eyes fixing on Jane Neal's stricken face.

'Four entirely separate people—you and your daughter are alike, but you are not the same. Two women but not all women. And here——' his hand closed on the photograph of Donald Neal '—*a* man—but not *all men*.'

Liz was stunned by the fact that he saw her mother's tears before she did, and with a warning glance alerted her so that this time she did move to her mother's side and take her hand—and to her surprise Jane did not resist.

'He—I——' Liz found the way her normally forcefully articulate mother was unable to string two coherent words together shockingly distressful.

'I know.' Richard's voice was infinitely soft. 'Believe me, I know.' And Liz suddenly found that she was swallowing down tears herself because in that moment she actually believed that Richard *did* understand the pain her mother felt. But a moment later Jane Neal's defences reasserted themselves.

'Perhaps you do, Mr Deacon—but if you do, then you'll also appreciate exactly why I want you to leave my daughter alone.'

'I——'

Liz couldn't wait to hear what Richard had been about to say because she could no longer keep silent. She wasn't sure that her mother had understood the full import of what Richard had said, but *she* had.

'That isn't the way to handle it, Mother,' she put in hastily, her voice firm with a new-found conviction because what she had to say was so very important. She didn't know where it would lead, whether it would change anything at all, but at last she was beginning to understand why she had agreed to meet Richard again, why she had continued to see him.

'I'm not you, Mother—and Richard isn't my father. We're two totally separate people and all men or all women can't be judged by what's happened between us. We're just a man and a woman and we have to work this out our own way.'

She didn't dare look at Richard as she spoke but she knew he was watching her; she could almost feel his gaze burning into her skin where it rested on her face. She was sure that, like her, he was remembering how he had accused her of letting her mother rule her life, and now she felt she was beginning to understand what he had meant.

'My father blighted your life, and you've dealt with that in the way that seemed best for you—but that isn't right for me—and I think perhaps you're beginning to see that, after all, it wasn't for you. But I won't let that happen to me. I'm a grown woman. You can't protect me from the world, and you have to let me do things my own way, make my own mistakes if necessary.'

Against her encircling arms she felt resistance and rejection stiffen Jane Neal's spine, but then, abruptly, her mother relaxed again.

'You must do as you think best.'

'That was more than I'd expected.'

Since they had left her mother's house, Liz had been in a state of tense anticipation of Richard's reaction to what had happened, but his first words came as something of a shock when she had expected some very close questioning over her mother's remarks about her own hopes for her career. From his tone she couldn't tell whether he had meant that just her mother's reaction had been more than he had expected or her own as well, but she didn't have time to consider the question because his next words were the ones she had been dreading.

'What the hell did your mother mean about your wanting to go freelance even before we were married?'

'I told you—it was just something I considered—but I changed my mind.'

She couldn't tell him why she'd changed her mind. That would mean admitting that when she'd seen the sort of home his mother and Eleanor provided for their husbands she had felt that she could never match up to their standards and run her own business as well so she had opted instead for a more secure, though less challenging, position in an office, believing that a nine-to-five job would give her more time to be the sort of wife she believed Richard wanted.

'I wouldn't have stopped you if that was——'

'No, I know you wouldn't!' Inner disquiet made Liz's voice sharper than she would have wished.

Thinking back over her feelings at Eleanor and Mark's dinner party the previous night, she had been forced to wonder whether, if she *had* gone freelance at the very beginning, and had made a success of it as she was now doing, she would have felt quite so inadequate when comparing herself with her mother and sister-in-law. Certainly, if she had had a job that absorbed her as much as hers did now, she might have been more understanding of Richard's dedication to his own work. But how on earth would she have managed all the social commitments that came from his job as well?

'But I decided that wasn't what I wanted to do after all.'

'Hmm...'

For one dreadful moment Liz thought that Richard wasn't going to accept her explanation, that he was going to question her further, but instead he turned a dark, inscrutable look on her and simply said quietly, 'We have to talk, Elizabeth—really talk. But not here. There are too many other pressures here. You said that you wanted a break, and I could certainly do with some time away. I'm going to be hellishly busy this week—but if you like we could go away at the weekend, book into a hotel somewhere.'

Last night she would have refused adamantly, doubting the reasons for his suggestion and not daring to face the possible consequences of her acceptance. But today, with so many new approaches to old problems to consider, Liz felt none of the flare of panic that the idea might earlier have aroused in her—and the diffidence of that 'if you like' had been strangely appealing, tugging at something in her heart.

'That might be a good idea,' she agreed slowly. 'Did you have anywhere particular in mind?'

Richard's eyes flicked to her face for a moment then back to the road again, his attention apparently concentrated on his driving.

'I think I know just the place,' he said. 'Leave it to me.'

CHAPTER NINE

'WE'RE here.'

Liz had been dozing, lulled by the movement of the car, her eyes closed, but now something in Richard's voice, a thread of unevenness that betrayed a tension he was trying to conceal, penetrated her sleepy mind and she sat up straighter, struggling to focus her blurred eyes on her surroundings.

But the next moment realisation hit her like the splash of icy water in her face, jolting her into stunned, disbelieving wakefulness as she took in the all too familiar skyline, the castle and the cathedral high on the hill above the town, and what little composure she had been able to gather fled completely.

'*No!*'

The word escaped on a gasp of horror. Not *Durham*! How could he? How *could* Richard bring her back here, knowing what painful memories such a trip would inevitably revive?

'No?' Richard echoed on a softly questioning note, and, strung as tight as a violin string, she rounded on him swiftly.

'How could you bring me *here*? How could you——?'

'Where else?'

Richard appeared totally unmoved by her outburst, his eyes fixed on the road before him, his profile etched against the window, stern and unyielding, offering no understanding of the tearing anguish that had ripped through her as soon as she had realised where she was.

'We agreed that we needed more time to get to know each other again—so what better place to do that than here, where we met the first time?'

137

Was he really as unaffected as he seemed? Had the sight of this once dearly loved place not touched him at all? Didn't he feel *anything* at returning to the place where they had once been so happy?

I *won't*! I will not stay here—I *can't*! The words formed in Liz's mind but she knew that she could never utter them. To do so would be to reveal the full extent of her feelings, the overwhelming sense of loss and despair that had assailed her at the sight of the familiar surroundings. And it would betray much, much more, would expose, finally and irrevocably, the realisation which had just broken over her like a tidal wave, flooding her mind so that it was impossible to think of anything else.

She still loved Richard. There was no denying it any more, not even to herself. *This* was why she had had to come with him on this weekend, not from any vaguely formed idea of getting to know him or making their final parting more amicable and civilised, but because the love she had felt for him in those long-ago days hadn't died as she had believed but, bruised and scarred, had retreated into some subconscious part of her mind until, fed by Richard's presence in her life over the past months, it had broken out again, as devastatingly powerful as ever.

But this time there was none of the glorious, mind-blowing delight, no delirious happiness, only a terrible sensation of loss and despondency that clawed at her savagely. She was older now, wiser, she hoped, and could no longer believe in the promise of that lifetime of love that Richard had once offered her. Experience had taught her that she didn't come first in Richard's life, that his job, his soaring ambition, held that place, and it was only as someone who could support him in those ambitions, who could act as his cook, housekeeper and hostess, that he wanted her. And in bed, she added with bitter honesty. Whatever else he had felt for her, his physical passion had never lessened—though now even that seemed to have died.

Vaguely she became aware that Richard had stopped the car and that he had turned and was watching her closely, noting the play of emotions that crossed her face, and Liz's heart clenched in panic at the thought of what he might have read there while her defences were down.

'Well?' he demanded sharply as she lifted her gaze apprehensively to meet his, finding his eyes as dark and impenetrable as the sea at night. 'Do we go on, or...?'

He left the sentence unfinished, but the words 'or forget the whole damn thing' were implicit in his tone of voice.

'What do you want to do, Elizabeth?'

What *did* she want to do? The emotional, sensitive part of her mind wanted to cry that she couldn't go on, that she couldn't bear to spend even an hour in Durham with all the memories that every street, every corner would bring back to her. But the other, more rational part warned her that to say so would be to reveal to Richard just how much those memories meant to her, to let him see into her heart and find there the love that she now desperately wanted to hide from him.

What would he do then? He had shown no sign of feeling anything for her other than casual friendship, with only those disturbing flashes of hastily concealed passion to ruffle the calm of his demeanour. Despondently she admitted to herself how little she now knew about this man who had once been her husband—who still was, in the eyes of the law at least. She had no real idea of his motives in continuing to see her like this, and when, on their second date, she had challenged him on that, he had simply parried the question by turning it back on her.

'I could ask the same of you. Why are *you* here with me?'

As Liz had spent a large part of the time since she had last seen him considering just that problem, the answer came to her tongue easily and unhesitatingly.

'We parted badly in the past and I don't want there to be that sort of ill feeling between us. We might not be able to live together any more, but that doesn't mean we have to turn this into some sort of private war.'

She had been so sure of her reasoning before, so convinced that her argument sounded rational, fair, and eminently adult—so why did she now feel dissatisfied with it, as if it was only a small part of the truth, and not a very important one at that? With a strange sense of apprehension knotting in her stomach, she waited for Richard's response. But he had simply nodded slowly, his face expressionless, his eyes disturbingly blank.

'Then we're both thinking along roughly the same lines,' he'd said quietly, and changed the subject.

'Elizabeth?' There was a distinct edge to Richard's voice now, one that pushed her into unguarded speech.

'Oh, well, you've booked the hotel now—it's too late to cancel.' With an effort she injected a fair assumption of carelessness into her voice, wanting to convey to Richard the idea that her earlier disturbed exclamation had been just a temporary upset. 'And it would be nice to see the old place again.'

And now there was something else she had to consider, something she had foolishly not stopped to think about before now, the belated realisation burning through her as she followed Richard from the car park and into the hotel. Just what sort of arrangements had Richard made for their stay? He had insisted that she left everything up to him, but he had never asked whether they would share a room or not, and it had never even crossed her mind that she should have stipulated which she preferred.

But wasn't the truth that she hadn't known what she wanted? Very probably she had subconsciously suppressed the question of single or double rooms because she hadn't wanted to make that decision. Deep down, she had wanted Richard to take matters out of her hands, had wanted him to book a double room if that was what he planned because then she would know that he felt *something* for her, some emotion stronger than the bland friendliness he had shown her over the past weeks, even if it was only physical desire.

As Richard had said, desire was the one thing that had never died between them even when they had been drifting far apart in other ways. From that first meeting at the wine bar she had known that the physical appeal Richard held for her was still there, in no way diminished by time and the unhappiness he had caused her.

Often, over the past few weeks, she had found herself watching the sure, confident movements of his hands, recalling the times when those hands had caressed her body, bringing it to tingling, glorious life under his touch, or perhaps in the middle of a conversation her thoughts had centred on his mouth, feeling in her imagination its demanding pressure against her own. The attraction of his strong, slim body still tugged at her like a magnet drawing a needle until she felt that, like a compass that always sought North, she must automatically be drawn to him if he was anywhere near. Every cell in her body leapt into instant response at his touch, a brotherly kiss on the cheek woke deep yearnings that she had to struggle to suppress in order to present a mask of uninvolved, unemotional friendliness to match the one he always showed to her. Whatever she felt about Richard himself, the sexual need he could arouse in her simply by existing hadn't died as it seemed to have done for him.

Or had it? Sometimes, looking into his eyes, Liz had seen in their darkness the flame of desire he couldn't disguise, though he never let it show in his face or his manner which was always unchangingly calm, polite and undemanding.

One thing was clear, however: the polite friendship and brotherly affection he had shown her over the past weeks were not enough. Physically at least, she was still enslaved by this man. She needed him, *wanted* him as much as she had ever done—more, in fact—and she could no longer maintain the objective, uninvolved façade that had been crumbling at the edges for some time. She had to face the knowledge that subconsciously she had agreed to this trip in the hope that as a result of spending forty-eight uninterrupted hours in each other's company, without the demands of Richard's job imposing a separation on them, she could break through the barriers with which Richard had surrounded himself, make him admit openly to the desire she had seen in those rare flashes, which he had ruthlessly refused to let show in any other way. She had come here in the hope of persuading him to make love to her.

'Mr Deacon?' The receptionist studied the list of bookings before her. 'Oh, yes—two single rooms for two nights—for yourself and Miss Neal.'

Liz's mental reaction was so violent that it actually rocked her on her feet and surreptitiously she put a hand on the desk to steady herself, watching through a whirling haze as Richard signed a form, accepted a key. *Single rooms*—and *Miss Neal*. Well, now she knew just what he felt—or, rather, didn't feel.

Somehow she managed to write her own signature, forcing herself to use the name that Richard had given though the tension in her hand, as if her body wanted to physically reject what she was doing, made her scrawl totally illegible.

'This way.'

If Richard had noticed her reaction he showed no sign of it as he led her into the lift and pressed the button for the third floor. Liz could only be thankful that he was conducting a casual conversation with the porter about the weather, his attention diverted for the moment so that she could sag back against the wall of the lift and concentrate on trying to regain some self-control, to suppress the searing pain that made her feel as if her heart were just a raw, bleeding wound.

Single rooms. Miss Neal. Only now did she realise how much it would have meant to her to have Richard book them into this hotel as man and wife, sharing a room. Instead, his actions had been a public declaration that he no longer considered them to be a couple. Even though, legally at least, she still had the right to the name Elizabeth Deacon, in Richard's mind she was Liz Neal, and, no matter how hard she tried to convince herself of the opposite, that meant that she meant nothing at all to him.

Numbly she followed the two men down the corridor, was vaguely aware of the porter depositing their bags in two adjacent rooms and accepting the tip Richard gave him. Then he left them, the moment she had been dreading arrived, and she was once more alone with this man whom she loved so deeply and who had just given her the clearest possible evidence of the fact that he did not love her.

'Well, I'll leave you to unpack.' After the bitter turmoil in her mind, Richard's relaxed, casual tone came as a shock to Liz. 'We could——'

Something inside Liz snapped and, not giving him a chance to finish his sentence, she rounded on him savagely.

'Why did you do that?'

Just for a second some violent emotion flickered in those blue-green eyes, then died like a candle extinguished by the wind, and the face Richard turned to her was coldly composed, all feeling blanked out.

'Do what?'

'You know what I mean! Downstairs—when we checked in——'

Liz couldn't form a coherent sentence; all the emotions she had experienced in those few short minutes seemed to have formed a tight knot in her throat and she couldn't force the words past it.

'Just what is bothering you, Elizabeth?' Richard enquired, his cool tones stinging like the flick of a whip.

'Miss Neal!' Driven beyond rational thought, it was all she could manage. *'Miss Neal!'*

Dark brows lifted in an expression of sardonic questioning and the perceptible tightening of Richard's mouth thinned it to a hard, unyielding line.

'And what's wrong with that? That is the name that you go by these days, isn't it?'

If he had slapped her hard in the face he couldn't have brought her up more sharply, more effectively. Liz found that she was actually gasping with shock.

'Don't tell me it's the single rooms you're objecting to.' With unnervingly sharp perception, Richard put his finger unerringly on the reason for her outburst. 'You surely didn't want us to share a——'

'You never even asked me what I wanted!' Liz took refuge in the fact that she could declare this grievance with some degree of conviction.

'I didn't have to ask—I knew what your answer would be.'

'Oh, so now you're a mind-reader, are you?' Pain, disappointment, and sheer, blind fury at his arrogant assumption that he knew what she wanted made Liz's tone bitterly sarcastic.

'Mind-reading doesn't come into it. You were the one who told me never to touch you again.'

Liz's face lost all colour, making her eyes huge and dark above ashen cheeks. She had forgotten that, forgotten how, in the heat of the moment, and still reeling from his rejection of her, she had flung those furious words at him. In the growing peace and new-found understanding between them, she had forgotten too that last night of their marriage, how Richard had used the physical power he had over her, using her body for his pleasure without a thought for her feelings. The memory of the anguish and desolation she had experienced then made her want to lash out at him, hurt him as she had been hurt.

'And when did that ever stop you? Wasn't that really what you had in mind for this weekend, to——?' The violent flash of Richard's eyes froze her tongue in her mouth.

'Now who's the mind-reader?' Liz flinched inside at the black irony of Richard's voice. 'But, tell me, just what *did* I have in mind for this weekend? To get you on your own and fling myself on you, to satiate my lust on your body at the very first opportunity? Oh, no, my darling Beth——'

Richard's personal version of her name that she had heard so often in the soft tones of love was now flung at her with a scathing contempt that burned her nerves as if it had been a powerful acid.

'—that wasn't the idea at all. I have no intention of letting myself be accused of rape again—once is enough!'

She'd *hurt* him, Liz realised with a devastating sense of disorientation. That wasn't anger in his voice, in his eyes, it was pain. Her unthinking words had actually pierced the armour of composure that he wore so easily that she hadn't even realised it had been there until the controlled mask had slipped for a moment, revealing the vulnerable man behind it.

So she had been wrong in her belief that Richard's choice of single rooms had been a deliberate rejection of her. He had had very different motives in mind—like the consideration of her feelings, a scrupulous regard for her thoughtless declaration that he was never to touch her again, something he had kept to rigidly ever since. Had she misread his behaviour completely, seeing indifference where in fact there was something more? If he hadn't felt anything then she couldn't have hurt him.

'Richard——' Liz's voice shook as much as the hand she lifted, reaching out to him hesitantly, her fingertips just touching his cheek.

'*No!*'

Richard repulsed the tentative gesture with a violent movement of his head, twisting away from her so that it was suddenly as if a vast, gaping chasm had opened up between them.

'No,' he repeated in a low, savage voice that tore at her heart. 'You may have forgotten what was said that day, but I certainly haven't—and I meant every word of it. It's that or nothing, Beth——'

Liz didn't think she had reacted to the shortened version of her name but the abruptness with which Richard stopped, the way his face closed up, blanking off all emotion as if a blind had suddenly come down behind his eyes, told her that he had remembered that she had forbidden him to use it. She was overwhelmed with a deep longing to tell him that it didn't matter, that to hear him call her Beth in the old, gentle way was what she wanted most in all the world. But before she could form the words Richard spoke again and the moment was lost.

'I think we both need some time on our own. You probably want to unpack and freshen up. I suggest that we meet for a drink before dinner—say, eight.'

The Richard hidden behind the armour, the one she had touched so briefly, was gone, and in his place once more was the controlled, politely distant stranger who was all he had let her see for so long.

'Would that suit you?'

It would suit me much more if you'd stay and talk this out, Liz told him in her thoughts, but she knew now was not the time to say the words. Every taut muscle in Richard's body, the clenched line of his jaw, his very stance, half turned towards the door as if he was already moving away from her, warned her that any attempt to take matters any further would be swiftly and possibly violently rejected. Perhaps when he had had that time on his own that he had mentioned, when he had had a chance to calm down, he would be prepared to listen to what she had to say. She could only pray that in that time he wouldn't also have a chance to build up the barriers again.

'That would suit me fine.' Liz had never thought of herself as an actress, but somehow she managed to hide the way she was feeling and keep her tone reasonably light. 'You're right—I would like to get on with my unpacking. I'll meet you in the bar, shall I?'

But as soon as the door had closed behind Richard she knew that unpacking was the last thing she wanted to do. Richard had been right about one thing, she did need some time on her own, time to think, to decide just what she was going to say when they met again. But she couldn't do that here, in this elegant but impersonal hotel room, knowing Richard was just next door. Pulling on her jacket, she grabbed her bag and headed for the door.

The grey clouds that had threatened earlier had vanished, leaving the sort of day that occasionally made December seem more like spring. Clear sunlight glowed on the mellow stone of Prebends' Bridge, warming it softly, as Liz leaned against the parapet, staring down at the winding River Wear below her, her thoughts inevitably going back to the way that only that morning she had realised that, in spite of everything that had happened, Richard still held that very special place in her heart. And now, here in their old haunts, Liz could only remember the happy days, wonderful, carefree times when she had felt as if she had been given the world.

So what had gone wrong? She had had no doubts at the beginning. Things had begun to change when Richard had finally achieved his ambition to set up on his own. That was when the demands of his work, and the entertaining that went with it, had begun to rule their lives. But it seemed that the harder she'd tried the more Richard seemed to move away from her.

And that was when he had started buying the presents. From the start, he had always remembered birthdays, Christmas, anniversaries, and he had often liked to surprise her with some small, carefully chosen gift, but now it seemed that as they drifted further apart the presents grew larger, more ostentatious and expensive: huge bunches of hothouse flowers where he would once have brought a delicate spray of the freesias she loved, French perfume, gold jewellery. And as he gave her more *things*, he gave her less of himself until she had felt like a kept woman, a housekeeper and bedmate who was paid in an unwanted shower of gorgeously gift-wrapped luxuries.

The growing tension between them had finally culminated in that terrible time before Christmas when she had locked him out of her bedroom, and from then on things had gone downhill fast. Because the worst thing was the way Richard hadn't seemed to care. He had continued as if nothing had happened, except that he had slept in the spare bedroom every night, shutting the door firmly against her. That situation had endured for a month or so, growing gradually more unbearable, what conversations they did have stilted and uncommunicative, dealing only with trivial matters, never coming close to the problems that were eating away at their marriage. And then——

Liz closed her eyes against the pain of that one, final memory. But it had to be faced. She had to remember it all if she was to decide what she was to do.

Eleanor and her husband had had dinner with them that night, and, determined to hide the fact that her life was in ruins, Liz had drawn on every shred of pride she possessed in order to present a brave face to the world. She had even bought a new dress, a fine silk sheath in kingfisher-blue that clung to every curve, its understated elegance enhanced by a heavy gold chain and matching earrings—Richard's Christmas present to her. Determined that everything should be perfect, she had worked harder than ever on the meal, and midnight found her aching with exhaustion but knowing that at least the evening had been a total success.

Richard had gone to the door to see Eleanor and Mark off and, left alone, Liz had begun clearing away, her movements slow and dragging as she put the dirty crockery in the dishwasher, thinking longingly of going to bed and the oblivion of sleep.

'Leave that.'

She hadn't heard Richard come back into the room, and his quiet voice coming from the doorway made her jolt upright in shock.

'It won't take a minute. I've nearly finished.' The effort she was making to appear calm, her self-control weakened by hours of trying to appear happy and relaxed when inside her heart was tearing apart, made her voice stiff and cold. 'You go up if you like.'

'I thought we could have a nightcap together.'

Just eight simple words in a voice that held no hint of threat, but to Liz it felt as if each word had been a separate dagger, stabbing deep into her soul.

In the past this had been their own private ritual. No matter how late it was, when their guests had gone and the debris of the meal had been cleared away, Richard would pour them both a drink, she would kick off her shoes and curl up in an armchair, and they would sit together, talking quietly, reviewing the evening, until they felt ready for bed. After the stress and strain of organising a dinner party, Liz had always loved those times, but lately the tradition had ceased, Richard going straight to bed without a word to her, so now his suggestion tore at her heart with the memories it awoke.

'I've poured you a brandy.' Richard lifted one of the glasses he held, offering it to her, but she shook her head slowly.

'I don't think so—I'm tired——'

'Beth——'

Whatever he had been about to say, Richard clearly thought better of it, pausing instead and taking a deep swallow of his own drink before continuing with what was clearly a complete change of subject.

'You're looking spectacularly beautiful tonight. Where did you find that sexy creation?'

'In a new boutique in the high street.'

Liz's response was purely automatic. The word sexy grated on her raw nerves, making her feel as if someone had dragged a piece of sandpaper over them. How long was it since she and Richard had made love? How many nights had she lain awake, aching in frustration and despair, knowing that he was only feet away from her and yet so far distant that they might have been at opposite ends of the earth? Never by so much as a look or a gesture had he betrayed any hint that he was feeling as she did.

'There!' She slammed the door of the dishwasher shut with unnecessary force. 'That's done! I'm off to——'

The sentence broke off on a startled cry. She hadn't seen Richard put the glasses down, hadn't heard him move, but suddenly he was behind her and her movement had brought her close up against him, throwing her off balance so that she swayed on her feet.

'Careful!'

Richard's hands came out to steady her, his touch cool and firm, but seeming to scorch her skin, making every nerve in her body feel as if it had come into contact with a live electric wire.

'Have a drink with me, at least, Beth,' Richard said softly, his grip on her arms tightening convulsively.

The look in his eyes made a coward of her. She had wondered how long the situation could go on as it was, knowing that a virile, sensual man like Richard wouldn't willingly endure a life of celibacy for long. At first she had seen their physical desire for each other as the potential answer to their problems; in the past so many of their quarrels had been made up in bed. But as the days had dragged past, with Richard remaining cold and aloof, that hope had died and she had withdrawn in on herself, trying to shut off her physical feelings as he seemed to be able to do so easily. So now she was amazed to see the flames of desire that burned in Richard's eyes and even more stunned by her own lack of response. He had waited too long. After weeks of trying to suppress the way she felt, now, at last, it seemed that she had succeeded.

'No, thank you,' she said stiffly, trying to twist away from him. 'I'm tired—I'm going to——' The last word caught in her throat, becoming an unintelligible croak.

'To bed,' Richard supplied for her. 'I think that's an excellent idea.'

But the implications behind his words were not what Liz had in mind at all. There was too much distance between them; too many things left unsaid—or, rather, the wrong things said and the right ones left unspoken. Over the past months—and more intensively since Christmas—Richard had become a stranger to her, and she couldn't go to bed with a man she didn't know, no matter how much she loved him—and, deep down, she was no longer even sure of that.

'Perhaps we could talk in the morning when we've both had some *sleep*.' Liz emphasised the last word deliberately. 'I—put fresh sheets on your bed today. You——'

Her voice failed her as she saw the dazed expression on his face as if she had actually struck him a blow. Then the unfocused look changed swiftly, devastatingly, and she flinched away from the savage fury that blazed in his eyes.

'You—*my* bed! Damn it, Beth, that isn't my bed and you know it! What happened to *our* bed—the one we used to share?'

Our—share—the words reverberated inside Liz's head, almost destroying what little remained of her self-control. She couldn't think, could only feel, and the sensation that filled her mind was one of searing anguish as if a cruel hand had gripped her heart and was slowly crushing the life out of it. For so long Richard had been indifferent to her needs, had ignored her existence, but now, when it suited him, he was making claim to her again.

'I think it's better this way, Richard.' Was that cold, proud voice really her own? 'I—prefer to sleep alone.'

A small, choking cry escaped her as Richard's grip tightened painfully, hard fingers digging into delicate flesh, bruising her skin.

'To hell with what *you prefer*! A marriage is two people and you've had it all your own way for too long. Tonight is for me—and I want this.'

With a rough movement he jerked her against the hard strength of his body, bringing his lips down on hers in a crushing, demanding attack that could only be called a kiss in the same way that a man-eating tiger was described as a big 'cat'. The pressure of his mouth forced Liz's lips open to the invasion of his tongue as his hands moved over her body in urgent, almost violent caresses that spoke eloquently of need and desire but nothing of love.

She didn't want this! Liz thought on a wave of shock and anger, her whole body stiffening in rejection, exerting every ounce of strength she possessed in an attempt to break away from Richard's hold. But her puny resistance was ineffective when pitted against Richard's physical dominance, her futile struggles seeming only to inflame his mood. He seemed like a man possessed, crushing her against him in a way that made her heart contract in panic.

'Richard—*no*!' she gasped when his mouth finally left hers, praying that the sound of her voice might penetrate the haze of fury and desire that filled his mind, restore him to some degree of rationality, make him aware of what he was doing.

'Richard—*yes*!' Richard muttered thickly as he pressed burning kisses against her cheek, her mouth, the slender line of her throat. '*Yes*, my lovely Beth! This is what I want—and if you're honest it's what you want too!'

'*No!*'

But it was a despairing cry, one that, even in her own ears, lacked any degree of conviction, and as soon as she heard it Liz knew that she could no longer deny what was happening to her, knew that she was losing her battle against him because now her own body had joined forces with Richard against her. It was acting independently of her mind, the long weeks of loneliness and longing catching up with her, so that, like a well-tuned instrument responding to the touch of a master-player, it was reacting instinctively to the touch of Richard's hands, the taste of his mouth, with the overwhelming force of need sharpened by long denial.

Her mind hazy with passion, she felt herself swung up into his arms, the kitchen door was kicked open, and Richard carried her swiftly upstairs into their bedroom.

'*This* is my room, Beth!' he declared as he laid her on the bed, his hands sliding up into her hair, twisting in the silken dark strands to hold her prisoner. 'This is where I belong—where *you* belong—with me! No more separate rooms, no more empty nights—you're my wife and I want you——'

The feeble protest Liz tried to make was crushed beneath the pressure of his lips once more, and from that moment she knew that she could no longer deny the rising crescendo of need that assailed her. The past, and how she would feel in the morning, no longer mattered. All that was real was here and now, with Richard's lips on hers, his hands on her body. She wanted him with her, wanted to feel his warmth and strength around her, inside her, and she did not resist as he eased the clothes from her body, his caresses suddenly changing, becoming more gentle, softly teasing, tantalising her with his delicate touch. As his fingertips brushed over her breasts a low laugh of triumph escaped him as he heard the moan of longing that she could not hold back.

'Yes, Beth—this is how it should be. This is where we really communicate.'

But Liz didn't want him to talk. His kisses and caresses were driving her into a frenzy of need, every moment he held off from the full consummation of their lovemaking was an agonising torment so that she reached up and caught his head in her hands, her fingers clenching in the darkness of his hair, dragging his face down to hers so that their lips met again.

Hearing Richard's harshly indrawn breath, feeling the shudder of response that shook his body, Liz knew that he was as out of control as she was, and gloried in the feeling of power that that brought. Instinctively she arched her body against his, mutely inviting the intimate invasion she so longed for, and as Richard responded to her unspoken invitation she thought that her mind would shatter with the force of the overwhelming delight of their shared passion.

After four years of marriage, their bodies were perfectly attuned to each other, every movement, every touch an intuitive response to the other's need, inciting further caresses, building the storm of need as it added to their pleasure. And as the primitive rhythm built upwards, soaring higher and higher, Liz thought that perhaps, after all, it had been worth that terrible month of separation when the end result was this spiralling, mind-shattering joy that finally devastated her with an explosion of ecstasy such as she had never known before.

Drifting slowly back to reality, her body still seeming to float in a warm, golden sea of happiness, Liz heard Richard's ragged breathing gradually slow, become regular and even again.

'That was how it should be, Beth,' he said in a voice still thickened by the storm of passion that had possessed him. 'That was why we're together, why sleeping in separate rooms is such a bloody stupid idea. I can never get enough of you, Beth, and I never will. I knew that from the moment I first saw you. I knew then that I just had to get that glorious body of yours into my bed—and keep it there. That's why I married you. You belong here, with me—and you know that. When it can be like this, nothing else matters.'

'Nothing else matters.' Richard's words were like a knife of ice slashing through the warm bubble that enclosed Liz. 'I just had to get that glorious body of yours into my bed... That's why I married you.'

Suddenly all the hidden fears that were buried in Liz's subconscious mind rose to the surface with the force of an erupting volcano. When Richard had asked her to marry him, she had believed that his actions were motivated by a love as strong as her own, and had accepted them as that, pushing aside the lessons she should have learned from her mother's experience, burying them under her own needs, her own longing for things to be as she thought they were.

Because love had had nothing to do with it. Richard had said that she had knocked him off balance, but his reaction had been physical, not emotional. He had never loved her, only wanted her—wanted her so much that he was prepared to marry her in order to get her. The overwhelming ambition that drove him was the only emotion he was capable of feeling. There had been nothing more, only Richard's calculated determination to get what he wanted out of life. Her mother had been right; all men *were* like her father—totally selfish.

Long after Richard had fallen asleep, Liz lay awake in the darkness of the night, forcing herself to come to terms with the fact that her marriage was over, or, rather, that it had never existed in the way she believed the word marriage meant. Richard had never actually lied to her, but he had known how she felt and had let her continue in her blind delusion. But now her eyes were wide open and she saw the truth at last.

And so, when Richard had gone to work the next morning, she had packed her bags and gone, leaving no note, but instead pulling off her wedding-ring and placing it in the centre of the pillow on Richard's side of the bed where he couldn't fail to see it. Knowing now as she did what he had wanted from her and their marriage, that seemed an appropriate place to leave the small, golden symbol of a love that had never existed.

CHAPTER TEN

THE bar was quite crowded by the time Liz made her appearance, but nevertheless her eyes still went straight to the table where Richard, sharply elegant in a charcoal-grey suit and crisp white shirt, sat alone, a look of brooding thoughtfulness on his face. At once a feeling like the fluttering of butterfly wings started up in the pit of her stomach. She had needed time to think, and it seemed as if, in the hours since she had left her room, she had done nothing but that—but she had come to no definite conclusion, and that thought made her steps hesitant and uncertain as she made her way across the room towards him.

Alerted by some sixth sense, Richard glanced up, getting to his feet as she approached, and Liz's heart contracted in immediate response to the attraction of his lean, lithe body in the perfectly tailored suit, the angular planes of his face in which those sea-coloured eyes were dark and enigmatically expressionless. But then Richard's gaze moved from her face to her body and a dramatic change took place, a flash like the flare of a match lighting in them, telling her that the decision she had made in her room half an hour earlier had had the effect she had anticipated.

The delicate peach of her dress was an unusual choice for her—normally she stuck to bright, clear colours that went so well with her dark colouring—but without vanity she knew that it suited her, throwing a soft, warm light on to her skin and making her eyes seem the colour of a dove's wing. The soft fabric clung to the lines of her body, emphasising every curve, and in spite of the fact that it was high-necked and long-sleeved she knew that the overall effect was more subtly sexual than any more blatant style.

She had bought the dress on impulse only the day before, and, if questioned, would have said that, seeing what the colour did for her, she couldn't resist it. But the truth was more complicated than that, as her realisation in the car on the way here had taught her. Subconsciously knowing that she was still deeply attracted to Richard, she had bought it for just this occasion—and to create just this effect. But, no matter how many times she considered the question, she still couldn't decide whether that response was one she wanted or dreaded.

'I'm sorry if I'm a bit late——'

Politeness decreed that she should say something, but deep inside her heart contracted painfully at the thought that once more they were back on the restricting path of careful politeness, once more pretending to be the strangers they could never really be.

For a brief moment her remark met with no response, then Richard gave an odd, jerky shake of his head as if he were waking from a dream and was having trouble clearing it from his mind.

'That's OK,' he said unevenly. 'I've only just got here myself.' A second later he had recovered himself completely, the strange roughness ironed out of his voice as he added, 'Would you like a drink?'

'I'd love one.' Liz's reply had the enthusiasm of strict honesty. She felt as if she were walking on eggshells, every nerve stretched tight in apprehension, and the thought of the relaxing properties of alcohol was infinitely welcome.

He hadn't asked what she wanted, she realised belatedly as Richard moved to the bar, but then it would be ridiculous to take the idea of being strangers so far as to pretend that he didn't know only too well what she liked. But there had been more to it than that. Richard had seemed almost glad to get away for a moment, like a man who had suddenly found a situation too much to handle and needed a breathing-space in which to collect his thoughts.

Which was exactly how she felt too, Liz reflected, her mouth taking on a wry twist at the thought that she had tried to spend the last few hours doing just that and never quite managing it.

'I've only just got here myself,' Richard had said, and his words had come as no surprise to her because when she had finally left Prebends' Bridge, her thoughts still every bit as confused as before—in fact, more so with the bitter memories of the last night of her marriage still in her mind—she had wandered through the narrow streets, not caring where her steps took her as she remained lost in her memories. When she had finally surfaced again it was to find herself, inevitably, on the far side of Palace Green, staring across at the imposing north front of the cathedral. It was there that Richard had proposed to her on a bright, clear day in March, a proposal she had accepted without any doubt or hesitation. How would she have felt if she could have seen into the future at that point?

As she turned to cross the square, Liz halted suddenly, her gaze going to the solitary masculine figure standing near the arch of the great doorway. Although his back was towards her, his eyes apparently fixed on the huge, ornate metal head that formed the Sanctuary Knocker as if he had thoughts of seeking refuge inside the cathedral itself, as long-ago escapees from justice had done, she knew immediately who it was—and that had raised the question of why Richard should be here, why, like her, his first instincts had been to visit the places that had so many memories for them both.

Liz wished that she could see his face, read from his expression what sort of thoughts filled his mind. Were they simply nostalgic, or, like hers, filled with the pain of loss and regret for the way the promise of the past had been destroyed by the path their lives had taken?

Or, a more severely realistic part of her mind added, was he in fact bitterly regretting the proposal he had made on that spot years before?

One thing was sure, and that was that after the way they had parted in the hotel she couldn't face him now. And so she had backed away, retreating as swiftly and carefully as she could, vanishing without Richard ever knowing that she was there.

But when Richard returned with her drink, curiosity, and a need to probe his reasons for that sentimental pilgrimage, overcame her reticence.

'You said you'd only just got here—have you been out, then?'

'Yes, I went for a walk. I wanted to stretch my legs after so long in the car.'

'Has the place changed at all?'

Liz didn't know why she kept her own trip out to herself; it was an instinctive reaction to Richard's non-committal comment which showed that he had no intention of telling her exactly *where* he had walked to—or why. Besides, when she was so unsure of his feelings, it was probably wiser not to reveal too much of her own inner thoughts. That would betray a vulnerability she wasn't yet ready to let him see.

'Not really—but then I never expected it would have. Durham has a sort of timeless quality about it. They can build a new shopping centre, or create a one-way system, but they can never really *change* it.'

Liz could only nod agreement, finding herself suddenly unable to speak. If only that timeless quality could have worked for them too. If only they could go back to being the people they had been in those first days in this town. But had Richard ever really been the man he had seemed then? And the truth was that time never stood still for anyone. She had to deal with what was here and now.

And what was here and now was that Richard's eyes, strangely dark and intent, were fixed on her as if they wanted to probe deep into her soul. The mesmeric force of his gaze held Liz's grey eyes transfixed.

'Why—why are you looking at me like that?'

She saw him blink hard, saw the immediate withdrawal her words caused, but his tone was carefully polite when he spoke.

'Because you're looking wonderful tonight. That dress really suits you.'

Liz managed a smiling inclination of her head in response to the quiet compliment, thankful that she was able to hide the whirlpool of confusion into which it had thrown her thoughts. In the bedroom upstairs, she had hesitated over wearing this dress, the memory of the last night of her marriage still so vivid in her mind, making her doubt whether she really wanted Richard to see her in it, to see her in any sort of sexual way at all. But that doubt clashed with the way she had felt when she had realised that Richard had booked single rooms, and in the end she had stuck to her original plan. And now the darkness of Richard's eyes, the huskiness of his voice, told her that the impact she had hoped for with the dress had been achieved beyond expectations—the problem was, how far did she want to take things?

It was a problem that fretted at her mind all through their meal and afterwards, when they lingered over coffee. It seemed as if fate had conspired with her memories to keep her in a permanent state of indecision as images of the past and a determination never to get caught in the trap of blind love again warred with the instinctive response of her body and mind to the potent force of Richard's physical presence.

And Richard himself only compounded the problem, seeming to have thrown off his darker, more abstracted mood, and set himself to being his most charming, entertaining self, providing the sort of fascinating, delightful and amusing company that she had so valued in the past.

Every one of Liz's senses seemed heightened, disturbingly aware of the lean, firm body in the immaculately fitting suit, the contrast between his dark hair and the gleaming white of his shirt, and the intriguing, changeable blue-green of his eyes. Emotionally, she had no idea where she stood, but one thing was very clear in her mind. She *wanted* this man, wanted him with a passion that dried her mouth, made her hands unsteady, and sent her voice into curious patterns, sometimes high-pitched and nervous, and at others deep and husky as if she had a painfully sore throat.

She would just go with the tide, she decided, let the evening—and Richard—go whatever way they would, and leave it all up to fate. So when at last Richard, with what she hoped was a note of reluctance in his voice, declared that perhaps it was time that they called it a night, she went up in the lift with him in a state of something close to suspended animation, not thinking, not feeling, not anticipating anything—until he paused at her door and said, 'Well, I'll say goodnight, Elizabeth, and thank you——'

'Goodnight!'

Liz was unable to bite back the exclamation and it escaped her before she had time to think whether it was wise. Her stomach clenched in apprehension as she saw the frowning, questioning look he turned on her. She didn't want the evening to end like this—in fact, she didn't want it to end at all—and that made her rush on awkwardly.

'I—wouldn't you like to come in for a minute?'

Richard took an inordinately long time to decide on his answer to that question, but at last he nodded slowly.

'If you're sure...'

Liz suddenly felt that she would scream with frustration if they pussyfooted around much longer, neither of them actually saying anything, but each of them knowing that the undercurrents were there, silent but immensely powerful. But then, what could she actually *say*? She couldn't just come out with it boldly, declaring, 'Richard, I don't know how you feel about this, but I would very much like you to make love to me.' Or could she?

'I'm quite sure,' she managed, knowing that she could at least commit herself that far.

She could have done this so much better. With a little forethought she could perhaps have bought a bottle of wine and suggested that they share it. That would at least have done something to ease the awkward preliminaries, because she couldn't pretend to herself that Richard had accepted her invitation just to *talk*. But then, earlier, she hadn't anticipated this moment, hadn't been able to make up her mind. In fact she had never actually *decided*; it was just that, in the moment Richard had said goodnight, she had known that she couldn't let him go like that, couldn't leave him with so many things left unsaid and all the night in which he could build the barriers securely up around himself again.

But how she wished he wouldn't prowl round her room like a caged animal. She was nervous enough already, and his restless movements were only making things so much worse.

'This is a very pleasant room,' Richard said at last and Liz hastily smothered a nervous desire to laugh. She had no doubt that Richard's own room was an exact mirror-image of this one and the determined effort he was making at some form of conversation brought her perilously close to hysteria.

'Yes, it is,' she managed in a voice that shook noticeably. 'I——'

Her voice died as she looked into Richard's face and saw the darkness of his eyes. For a second they stared at each other, the silence between them seeming so taut and tangible that Liz felt it would shatter into tiny fragments if either of them moved. Then, abruptly, Richard swung round, heading for the door, flinging some inaudible phrase at her over his shoulder as he left the room.

Stunned and thoroughly disconcerted, Liz could only stand silently, her eyes still on the space where he had stood. What was happening? Downstairs, with his dark eyes watching every move, responding to every smile, every gesture, she had believed that, like her, he had thought that there was only one possible conclusion to the evening, but as soon as she had invited him into her room he had tensed up, seeming to withdraw in on himself. Was it possible that Richard could be as nervous as she was herself? *Richard?*

She hadn't time to consider the matter further because a few moments later Richard was back in the room.

'I bought this earlier,' he said, lifting one hand to show her a bottle of wine. 'We might as well share it—as a nightcap.'

Did he, like her, catch the echoes that phrase brought with it that shivered on the air—memories of the last night they had shared as man and wife? Liz's mind seemed to slide out of focus at the thought, and with the realisation of the way his words echoed almost exactly her own thoughts a few minutes earlier. *Could* he be nervous?

But watching his swift, efficient movements, his relaxed face as he opened the bottle, Liz was forced to reconsider her judgement as a foolish delusion born of the hope that Richard still felt something for her. 'I bought this earlier,' he had said, so, unlike her, *he* had been planning ahead.

Only that afternoon he might have angrily denied the idea that he had brought her to Durham with the intention of seducing her, but perhaps the things she'd said, the consternation she hadn't been able to hide on discovering that he had booked separate rooms for them, had changed his mind, made him realise that her angry command never to touch her again was no longer quite so adamantly meant. A flame of anger flared inside Liz at the thought that, seeing her weakening, he had calculatedly planned just this very scene. It was no wonder that he had been such delightful company all evening, the charm laid on with a trowel because every word, every gesture had been leading up to this moment.

'I'm afraid I didn't think about glasses.' There was a faint tremor of self-derisory laughter in Richard's voice. 'We have a choice between the ones in the bathroom or these teacups—and it doesn't seem right to drink Chablis from them.'

'The bathroom ones it is, then.' Liz was on her way to fetch them as she spoke.

It was only when she actually had the glasses in her hands that she paused, realising what was happening to her. Where had the anger gone? What had happened to her indignation at the thought of his deliberate scheming? It had died in the moment he had turned that boyishly sheepish grin on her, something in the wry smile tugging at her heart and driving away the hostile emotions. Besides, she admitted rather shamefacedly, how could she blame him when she had had much the same thought in her own mind?

And *Chablis*—Richard had chosen her favourite wine, the one whose dry, light taste she loved most in the world. So what interpretation should she put on that? Was it just one more part of a scheme to weaken her defences in order to seduce her, or was there more—or, rather, less—to it than that? Had he simply meant to please by choosing the wine that would give her the most enjoyment?

'Your glasses, sir.' The elaborate flourish with which she set them down on the dressing-table was carefully designed to hide her confusion, the uncertainty he must see in her face if he looked at her directly. 'The best crystal money can buy,' she added with deliberate irony at the fact that the tumblers were in fact the usual thick, heavy glass.

'Nothing but the best for us,' Richard agreed, following her lead easily. 'I think that the wine is chilled to perfection, so if madam will just be seated...'

The touch of the guiding hand he placed under Liz's elbow sent hot waves of response searing through her, making her heart thud unevenly so that she felt sure Richard must see the wave of colour that washed her cheeks. And now she knew why her anger had vanished so swiftly. There was no room for it in her mind where all she could feel was the quivering sense of her whole body coming alive, awakening to his touch as a flower to the sun. How could she feel anger towards Richard for wanting what she too had wanted so much? And yet there was still a shadow of pain at the thought that, on his part, it was all calculation and little feeling.

'Your wine, madam——' Richard presented the glass with a flourish that matched her own earlier, something that, taken together with the fact that his eyes didn't quite meet hers, made her reflect on the fact that perhaps, after all, his motives for the playacting were the same as hers had been.

'Thank you, Jeeves.' Her private thoughts made it a struggle to inject the right degree of lightness into her voice, and she had to impose a ruthless control on herself to hide the betraying tremor that threatened to reveal her inner tension.

Why were they playing around like this? she thought, sipping the cool wine gratefully. Why didn't Richard just come out and say what he wanted?

Why didn't she? Her mind threw the question at her with devastating suddenness so that her hand clenched convulsively on her glass. She wanted his lovemaking every bit as much as he wanted her—or, as much as she *thought* he wanted her, cold reason added disconcertingly. She was acting on pure instinct. Richard hadn't actually said or done anything—he hadn't even tried to kiss her. He had even been about to say goodnight and go to his own room before she had rushed in with her clumsy invitation. *She* had been the one who had enticed him in here. Her body was so hypersensitive to the appeal of his, her own need and longing so powerful that perhaps she was simply projecting those desires on to Richard. Or perhaps, seeing as she had been the one to make the first move, he was simply following her lead, as she had done in their fooling about the glasses, and he was waiting for *her* to take things a step further.

So why didn't she? When she had first known him, and in the early days of their marriage, it had been so easy. A touch, a smile, a kiss had been all that was needed; neither of them had ever needed to speak, words had been totally superfluous.

Richard had moved to the opposite side of the room, his glass in his hand, and was studying the print of the cathedral that hung on the wall.

'I don't think I could ever get tired of this place,' he said quietly, his eyes still on the picture. 'I'd be quite happy to stay here like this forever.'

Like this—did that mean with her? Liz got to her feet and, hoping that her movements looked casual and relaxed, she strolled over to stand beside him.

'St Cuthbert's church—the ''grey towers of Durham'',' she murmured softly, quoting Sir Walter Scott's description of the city.

'''Half church of God, half castle 'gainst the Scot'',' Richard completed the quotation then suddenly swung round to face her, a smile tugging at the corners of his mouth. 'Do you remember how your mother condemned Cuthbert as the original male chauvinist pig?'

'She was furious when she went into the cathedral and discovered the line of marble by the font which marked the point beyond which women weren't allowed to go,' Liz agreed, laughter and the way his smile had affected her making her heart seem to be beating high up in her throat, combining to make her voice sound breathless and uneven. 'We tried to tell her that it wasn't Cuthbert who actually built the church, but she insisted that he was the cause of it because of the legend that he disliked women so much.'

Then, because the thought of her mother awoke disturbing memories of the previous weekend and the scene in Jane Neal's kitchen, she changed the subject hurriedly.

'One thing's sure, those monks wouldn't have coped very well with women today.'

'Can any man?' The quietly spoken words stopped Liz dead in her tracks and she stared deep into Richard's eyes, seeing how their clear, changeable colour had darkened to a deep shade of blue.

'What do you mean?'

For a moment she thought he wasn't going to answer her, but then he lifted his shoulders in a shrug that dismissed his reservations as unnecessary.

'Women have made it only too plain what they *don't* want from men—and quite rightly too—but sometimes, when the old, traditional breadwinner and protector roles have gone, it's hard to know what to put in their place— to know what you really want.'

Liz's mouth was suddenly dry and she wetted her lips nervously with her tongue. Was he aware of that revealing slip, that change from 'women' to *'you'*? And did that mean as much as she wanted it to? She didn't know, and right now she didn't really care. Rational thought was completely suspended in her mind and instinct took over as, taking a step forward, she looked deep into his dark eyes.

'I know what I want from you right now,' she said in a voice that was amazingly firm and confident in spite of the fact that she was feeling as if a whirlwind had invaded her mind.

Richard looked as if he had suddenly been hit very hard, a stunned expression clouding his eyes as he blinked hard.

'Beth——' he began hoarsely, then stopped, seeming unable to continue, and the vulnerability revealed in the uncharacteristic hesitancy tugged at Liz's heart.

'Kiss me, Richard.'

The few seconds while he still held back seemed to drag out interminably, and pain tore at her in a sudden moment of intense realisation of just how much this man meant to her. Surely she hadn't found him again only to lose him once more?

'Richard——'

In another moment she would have turned and fled, devastated by the way she had revealed her deepest feelings to a man who didn't care for her at all. But then—and she was never quite sure who moved first, Richard or herself—she was in his arms, held so tightly that she felt her bones might actually crack under the pressure, and kissed hard, greedily, as if Richard had been starved of physical contact for years.

Which was exactly how she felt too, and, like a starving person faced with a banquet who couldn't decide where to start, so now she found that she didn't know what she most wanted—to kiss him, touch him, caress him— and her lips moved over his face in desperate, snatching kisses, her hands tangling with his as they reached for each other, fired by a need that was burning them up. Richard's caresses were as urgent as her own, setting every nerve alight, making her heart beat so fast that it sounded like the roar of thunder in her ears and she was only vaguely aware of Richard easing her backwards until her legs came up against the edge of the bed and she sank down on to it, her hands linking behind his neck, pulling him with her until he lay half across her.

Liz gloried in that hard weight pinning her down. This was how it had always been in the past, how they had broken through the barriers that had come between them. Later, when the inferno of passion had burned itself out, they would be able to talk, but for now this wordless, most primitive form of communication was all that was necessary.

A choking cry of delight escaped her as Richard's searching hands found her breasts and closed over them, his thumbs moving in tantalising circles that had Liz writhing in delight.

'Yes, Richard, yes!' she gasped. 'This is what I want—what I need from you——'

'No!'

The sound of Richard's voice, hard and sharp, broke into the delirium that filled her mind, shattering it like glass when a stone hit it, so that she froze into sudden stillness. A moment later he had wrenched himself away from her, flinging himself half across the room with the force of his rejection of her, to stand, dark and ominously threatening, his hands clenched into tight fists at his side, every muscle in his body taut and lines of hostility etched into his face.

'Richard...?' Liz's voice quavered painfully as she slowly levered herself up, her black hair in disarray, her face ashen with shock, her eyes just dark pools of loss.

'I said no!' Richard's savage tone seemed to cut into her heart like a knife. 'I told you, Beth, I don't want this any more, not——' He caught up what he had been about to say. 'I *don't want this*!'

He couldn't make it any clearer than that, Liz thought on a wave of bitter anguish, the sour taste of despair in her mouth. He didn't want her—not even physically. It seemed she had read the signs all wrong—but she had been so sure. *He didn't want her.* The words drummed inside her head, beating against her brain as she forced herself to accept the truth though she felt as if her heart were tearing apart.

'Richard——' she began shakily, not knowing what she was going to say, but it was as if the sound of her voice was more than Richard could bear.

'No!' His hands came up before his face in a disturbingly defensive gesture. 'This weekend was a mistake, Beth—it should never have happened. We'll go straight home in the morning.'

'But——'

But Liz was speaking to empty air. Richard had already gone, the sound of the door banging to behind him seeming to emphasise his total rejection of her. Liz curled up on the bed, folding her arms around herself as if by doing so she could keep back the pain. And, although she knew it was hopeless, her mind would not let go of the thought that, even in the middle of his savage declaration that he didn't want her, Richard had still called her Beth.

CHAPTER ELEVEN

'LIZ!'

Eleanor's voice over the phone sounded sleepy and disturbed—as well it might, Liz reflected ruefully, seeing as she had been dragged from her bed at seven o'clock on a Sunday morning to answer a frantic call from her sister-in-law.

'Oh, Nell, I'm sorry to bother you like this, but I didn't know who else I could turn to. I have to talk to someone who knows Richard——'

After Richard's departure the previous night Liz had lain on the bed for a long time, feeling emotionally bruised and battered, trying to work out what had gone wrong. She had been so sure that Richard had wanted to make love to her—that that was why he had accepted her invitation to come into her room. Had she imagined all that? But she had felt his response when he had kissed her—that had not been imagination. She knew Richard well enough to know that he had been every bit as aroused as she had, so what had driven him to reject her so violently?

'I don't want that any more,' he had said, his eyes dark and stony, the muscles in his jaw tightly clenched, 'not——'

That 'not' had Liz suddenly freezing, stilling her restless tossing and turning as a memory surfaced in her mind, a picture of Richard speaking exactly those same words just a few short weeks before.

'I don't want that any more—not without the rest of you. It means nothing that way.'

So had that been rejection that had turned his eyes so dark and cold, or——? Recalling the tension in Richard's body, the way his hands had clenched at his sides, Liz suddenly felt cold all over at the thought that Richard had looked for all the world like a man in the grip of some intense pain, one he was struggling to control, her mental confusion growing as, loud and clear as if he had actually been in the room, she heard his voice saying, '*Your* marriage...! What about *our* marriage, Beth?'

Had she been wrong all along? Had she seen Richard's careful politeness, the distance he kept between them, as coldness and indifference, when in fact he was fighting to hide other feelings, ones he felt that *she* wouldn't want him to show? And now, when she was least able to cope, the things Eleanor had said when she had tried to persuade Liz to write to Richard came back to her.

'I think he's desperately lonely,' her sister-in-law had said, 'and I'm terrified that he'll go completely off the rails. He's working too hard, he's not eating, and I'm damn sure he's not sleeping too.'

Liz had seen with her own eyes the physical changes in Richard, the loss of weight, the way his skin was drawn tight over his facial bones, the shadows under his eyes that made him look like a man who had lost something very precious to him and who was totally devastated by that loss. But he had denied Eleanor's story, had laughed off the things she had said—so what was the truth? In the darkness of the early morning Liz had finally decided that she needed help—which was why she now found herself pouring out the whole sorry tale to Eleanor.

'I still love him, Nell,' she finished chokingly. 'I love him every bit as much as when I married him—but I don't know what he's feeling—I'm not sure I ever did.'

'Have you asked him?' Eleanor's question brought Liz up sharp, her eyes staring sightlessly at the wall.

'Tell me about your marriage, Elizabeth,' Richard had said. 'I'm willing to tell you about my marriage—you've only got to ask.'

But, convinced that her love for him had died, sure that she hated him, she had rejected that tentative opening, declaring that she didn't want to talk about anything.

'I don't think he'd tell me if I did,' she said defensively.

'That's possible. My brother was never very good at expressing his feelings—but that doesn't mean he doesn't have any. He's very like my mother in that. I know Ma can come across as cold and unfeeling, but she was brought up to believe that any show of emotion was un-ladylike, and so, although she adores my dad she doesn't show it—not in public anyway. She has the same problem with anyone she cares about so she finds other ways of showing how she feels—like preparing spectacular meals, keeping the house immaculate, giving wonderful presents——'

Presents. The rest of Eleanor's words faded to a haze as Liz recalled the presents with which Richard had showered her, presents she had come to hate because she had thought they were just meaningless gestures. But since he had come back into her life he hadn't given her a thing—not even flowers. Was that because he no longer cared or because he wanted to give her something much more important?

'Richard takes after Ma—and I think that, being so much like her, he needed someone who could *give* more easily. I really thought he'd found that someone in you.'

'But, Nell, I tried! I tried so hard. I wanted to be the perfect wife——'

'Too perfect,' Eleanor put in crisply. 'Good lord, Liz—those dinner parties—they were out of this world. And the house—the way——'

'But——' Liz's head was reeling. 'But *you* do that! You—and your mother—are always so organised, so——'

Eleanor's swiftly drawn-in breath dried the words in her throat. 'Oh, Liz, don't tell me that you modelled yourself on me!' Liz stared at the telephone receiver in consternation, disturbed by the urgent note in Eleanor's voice. 'Don't you know I cheat like hell?'

'Cheat?' Liz echoed faintly.

'I work because I want to—but I can't do everything. So I have a superb "daily" who looks after the house, we have a maintenance contract——'

'But the meals you gave us——'

Eleanor's laugh had a shamefaced note in it. 'I didn't make them. I know this wonderful woman who just loves to cook and does it superbly. If I'm having a dinner party I just tell her what I want and she does the rest—the cooking, the table—everything. I've completely opted out of the domesticated bit—I have to—otherwise I'd never have any time or energy left to give to Mark and Rachel, and they're the ones who really matter—the rest is only show.'

'But I thought...'

Liz's voice died as she thought back over what her sister-in-law had said, a cold shiver running down her spine as she looked back at her own marriage. Had she devoted all her time and energy to the things Eleanor described as 'only show'—in her attempt to be the perfect wife?

'I thought you knew all this, otherwise I'd have told you the truth then—but you did everything so well that I believed you wanted to do things yourself. Richard thought so too——'

'Richard thought——' Liz's mind wouldn't function coherently enough even to enable her to repeat what Eleanor had said.

'Yes, he thought that because your mother was such an independent and determined woman that you wanted to be like her. He tried to help, but it seemed you didn't want that and he was afraid you'd think he was implying you couldn't cope if he persisted.'

Once more Liz heard Richard's voice inside her head. 'Sometimes, when the old, traditional breadwinner and protector roles have gone, it's hard to know what to put in their place—to know what you really want.' Had she been, subconsciously, so indoctrinated by her mother's belief that a woman could handle anything that she had determined to do just that, and in doing so had left no time for Richard, had cut him out? Suddenly she knew with a desperate certainty that she had to find Richard and talk things out—if he would let her.

'Nell, I have to go.' She couldn't explain further but there was no need; her sister-in-law had understood intuitively.

'Of course you do. Give Richard my love.'

As she had been awake since six, waiting anxiously for the first possible opportunity to ring Eleanor, Liz was already dressed, so now it was the work of a minute to make her way to Richard's room, but to her consternation she found that his door was ajar, as if at some point Richard had simply let it swing to, not bothering to check that the lock had actually caught. Hesitantly she pushed it open, peering nervously into the room.

There was no one there. At first, seeing the empty room, Liz's heart seemed to stop beating at the thought that, after the events of the previous night, Richard had simply packed his bags and gone. But then she noticed the small, unmistakable signs that the room was still occupied: a hairbrush on the dressing-table, the tie he had worn last night tossed carelessly on to a chair, a pair of shoes beside the bed, and her breath escaped on a heartfelt sigh of relief.

But *where* was Richard? As her gaze took in the bed, its dishevelled state clear evidence of the fact that Richard had spent a night as disturbed and sleepless as her own, Liz suddenly knew with a rush of absolute certainty just where he would be. After all, hadn't she gone to the same place yesterday when she had needed to think things over?

A weak, wintry sun was struggling vainly against the heavy grey clouds as Liz made her way out of the hotel but she was impervious to the cold, unable to run fast enough, her mind buzzing with all that Eleanor had said, all that she had discovered about Richard—and herself.

'A marriage should be give and take'—her own words came back to haunt her. *Give and take*—and she had believed that in their marriage she had been the one to do all the giving, with Richard seeming to take everything she had to offer. But she had never really understood how he was *trying* to give, the significance of those presents she had so misunderstood—the gifts she had, metaphorically, flung in his face, condemning them as meaningless gestures.

Because now, with her mind suddenly clear and calm, she could see just how much Richard had given in his own way. He had been aware of the hopes she had had for her life, hadn't wanted her to take the job in the office in the first place, but had urged her to look for something much better. *She* was the one who had kept her dream of going freelance from him, had convinced him that she was happy as she was, and that he should concentrate on achieving his own ambitions—so she had no right to complain when he took her at her word. And hadn't her own experience of being self-employed over the past year taught her just how much setting up your own business demanded?

There were other things too—those rows about the housework, which she had taken as meaning that he didn't care when in fact he had wanted to spend more time with her—and that dreadful Christmas when she had locked him out of her room... The scene replayed itself in her head now like images from a film—a film formerly only half understood, but now seen with a whole new perspective.

'I *want* you to come with me. I *want* you to be there,' she had thought that Richard had said, and, overtired and over-sensitive, she had taken his words as an autocratic command, a declaration that, as his wife, her place was at his side. Now, with hindsight, she could recall the real emphasis that had escaped her then: 'I want *you* to be there.'

And why hadn't she heard him properly the first time? Why had she been so exhausted that her judgement was clouded and faulty? Because she had worn herself out trying to be the woman she had thought Richard wanted her to be, and had thrown herself into the role with the same sort of unthinking determination that had ruled her mother's life. But she had been too influenced by her mother, instead of simply being herself. That was what Richard had tried to tell her when he had shown her and her mother those photographs.

And now, with Eleanor's question, 'Have you asked him?' still sounding in her ears she could see that *she* had decided that that was what he wanted, she had never stopped to think, or ask if that was true, to find out whether, like Mark Baldwin, he would have been happy with something much simpler.

'Oh, Richard, I'm sorry—sorry—sorry!' Liz muttered the words aloud as she rounded the last corner and skidded down the stony slope that lead to Prebends' Bridge, coming to an abrupt halt as she saw the dark, still figure leaning against the wall, staring down at the river.

This time, Liz could have no doubts about the sort of thoughts that filled his mind, the weary despondency on his face told its own story, driving away her own nervousness and giving her the courage to approach him and lay a tentative hand on his arm.

'Richard, we have to talk,' she said softly.

Richard spun round, his eyes, dark and shadowed, going to her face as if he couldn't believe that she was real.

'Beth!' The rough, shaken huskiness of his voice tore at her heart, the feeling intensifying unbearably as, with an obvious effort, he hastily corrected himself. '*Liz*—what——?'

'No,' Liz put in hastily, instinct giving her the words to reach him. 'Not Liz—*Beth*!'

'Beth?' Richard echoed uncertainly. Then he shook his dark head in denial of the implications of that name. 'No, not Beth. Beth is—was—my wife.'

'And still is!' Liz's voice rose sharply, taking on a desperate intonation. He seemed so far away from her, and suddenly she was afraid that he was *too* far away, that she would never reach him. 'Richard, I'm still your wife—or I want to be—if you want me.'

That got through to him; his head went back sharply.

'If I want you! If I—oh, lord, Beth, I've always wanted you from the moment I first saw you!'

Suddenly his hands came out, grabbing hold of her arms and pulling her hard up against him as his lips, passionate and fiercely demanding, came down on hers. Liz met his kiss willingly, knowing that for the moment words were not enough, that this instinctive, basic form of communication was what was needed to penetrate the defences he had put up around himself, and feeling her response Richard changed his kiss from one of desperation to a gentler, more inviting caress, one that flooded her body with a sweet, glowing longing so that she felt as if she were melting into his arms, losing all her doubts and fears, all the pain of their separation in this one glorious embrace.

'Beth——' Richard's voice was low and shaken when he finally lifted his head to look deep into her eyes. 'What's all this about?' To her distress he took a step backwards, away from her. 'What is it you want?'

On the last words his tone had hardened noticeably, his first, instinctive reaction weakening as rational thought returned and he retreated behind the barriers once more. But he had called her Beth, and he hadn't released her—though Liz doubted if he was aware of the way his hands still gripped her arms—and that was enough to give her the courage to meet his searching gaze with some degree of confidence.

'I want *you*—I always have,' she said firmly and clearly, and caught the sudden flare of raw, unconcealed emotion in his eyes before the rigid control snapped back into place and blanked it off again.

'I told you——'

'Yes—I know,' Liz rushed on, not giving him time to finish the sentence. 'I know you don't want an affair—something that's just physical—sex without love. I know that—and it's not what I want either.'

'Then what——?'

Tears stung Liz's eyes at the sight of the urbane, charming, articulate Richard Deacon so completely at a loss for words.

'I want what we used to have—I want the love we shared—the marriage—the——'

But Richard had caught one particular word and he pounced on it sharply. '*Love*, Beth—you said love——'

And suddenly his eyes were no longer clouded and dull but clear and searching, seeking the answer he needed in her face. '*What* are you trying to say?'

'That I love you, Richard—I always have. I just got a little lost along the way.'

'We both did,' Richard said soberly. 'What happened, Beth? Where did I go wrong?'

'No—not you.' The need to wipe that look of doubt and self-reproach from his face made the words tumble out like a rushing stream. 'We *both* lost touch—we got bogged down in our jobs, earning a living, setting up home, and we forgot to talk about the things that mattered.' She paused, drawing a deep breath. 'A marriage should be give and take, Richard—but you also have to learn what the other person wants so that you know how to give.'

'And you have to see what the other person's giving before you can take it.' Richard nodded, his quiet response sending a shaft of delight through Liz at the realisation that he had empathically understood exactly what she was trying to say.

'I thought you wanted the sort of wife your mother and Eleanor are—an elegant hostess, the perfect home-maker, a cordon bleu cook——'

'Cordon bleu cook!' Richard's laughter had a shaken edge to it. '*Nell!* Beth——'

'I know,' Liz put in. 'That is—I know *now*,' she added, determined to be scrupulously honest, 'I rang Eleanor and she told me how she does it—but I didn't know then. I was nervous, and I felt inferior to your mother and sister. They seemed so super-efficient and I thought I'd never match up to them. And those dinners seemed so important to you that I wanted to do things properly, as your mother——'

'If I'd wanted things to be as my mother organised them, I'd have stayed at home, as a bachelor! Beth, I didn't marry you for your skill as a hostess or a cook— I wanted *you*. Do you think I'd have given a damn if you'd paid someone to do it all as Nell does—or simply served beans on toast? I invited people to dinner be-cause I wanted to build up my business contacts, yes— but most of all because I wanted people to meet my beautiful, intelligent, wonderful wife.'

Liz felt as if her thoughts were whirling round in her head. She had thought she'd understood everything, but she hadn't anticipated this.

'I was so proud of you—so proud to be with you, that you'd chosen to marry me—and I wanted all the world to know it.' The light of that pride shone in Richard's eyes now—and it was meant for her alone.

'And I thought it was all just to impress potential clients.'

'Bloody hell, Beth—no! How could you ever think that?' Richard looked deep into her face and his expression sobered abruptly. 'I didn't tell you, did I?' he said flatly. 'Beth, darling, I'm sorry—I'm afraid I'm not very good at expressing my feelings.'

He sighed deeply, raking one hand through the dark waves of his hair.

'I remember Nell laying into me after you left——'
The twist of pain on his finely shaped mouth had Liz
reaching for his hand to hold it tightly. 'She said I'd
never shown you how I felt—never fully expressed my
love for you. I told her she didn't know what she was
talking about—that I'd never stopped giving you tokens
of my appreciation——'

'The presents,' Liz supplied quietly when he broke off.
Richard nodded, giving a small, rueful laugh.

'Typical male—I thought that if you gave a woman
pretty things—flowers, perfume—the traditional trap-
pings of romance as advertisers would have us believe—
then she'd know that you loved her. It wasn't until you
accused me of only giving you *things* that I realised that
those presents meant nothing unless I told you that I
loved you as well.'

'But you can't blame yourself totally for that. You
never learned the emotional vocabulary you needed—
your mother——'

'Taught me to believe that giving things was the way
to express my feelings.' Once more that lop-sided, self-
derisory grin surfaced. 'Men may want to change, Beth,
love, but I'm afraid that the strong, silent type is still
very much in evidence.'

'And I didn't tell you how insecure I felt—that that
was why I didn't feel up to taking on a better job—I
didn't even tell you about my dreams of going freelance
because I felt I couldn't cope.' Liz couldn't let him
shoulder all the blame for what had happened. She had
been at fault too. 'And I just compounded the problem
with my superwoman act.'

'I wouldn't have minded so much if you'd let me help.'

'But I wanted——'

The words died on her lips as she looked back at the
past with a mind now clear of the clouding, distorting
effects of her own assumptions and saw how Richard
had wanted to help—how often he had tried to share the
jobs with her. In the beginning he had always come into

the kitchen, had taken on some task, but, trying too hard, being too much the perfectionist, and strung up with nervousness at the thought of trying to meet her own over-exacting standards, she had frequently snapped at him, criticised him. How many times had she exclaimed impatiently, 'Oh, I'll do it myself!'? It was no wonder he had given up in the end.

'You didn't seem to need my help in any practical sense, and, knowing your mother, I thought you might be insulted by my attempts—that you'd think I was implying you couldn't do it without me so I backed off. In the end it got so I didn't know how to reach you. You didn't want the presents, you didn't want my help—you were so independent that I didn't see how you could ever need me at all.'

And he had wanted to be needed; he had wanted desperately to give her something of himself. A wave of distress broke over Liz as she recalled how she had thought that Richard didn't know how to give, the way she had accepted her mother's accusation that, like all men, he was too hard, too selfish to care about anyone but himself. But she hadn't given him a chance. The only time that she had let down her own private barriers against the idea of being thought a weak woman had been on the day when she had had a migraine, and then Richard had been all kindness, all gentleness. He had cared for her so generously that day, but she had been too stubborn, too blind to appreciate what he was doing, and instead had seen his behaviour as a threat.

'In the end it seemed as if there was only one way I could touch you—both literally and metaphorically—and that was in bed. That was the only time you seemed to need me—but then you locked me out of our room——'

'I thought you didn't care about that.' It was just a low whisper, barely audible, but Richard caught it.

'Not care! Beth, if you only knew the struggle I had not to break that damn door down that night—and every other night afterwards. I'd always thought of myself as a reasonably civilised and liberated man, but at that point the primitive caveman in me very nearly took control, and I had to fight myself every moment of the day to suppress it. I told myself that you just needed peace and quiet and time on your own, that if I left you alone you'd come back to me—and anyway I had no damn right to demand that you slept with me if it wasn't what you wanted.'

Richard's hands clenched on Liz's, communicating the way he was feeling through the power of his grip.

'Hell—it nearly killed me to keep my hands off you when I wanted you so much. I saw making love as the only way I had left of expressing the way I felt about you—I was too stupid to realise that simple words would do—but you were so cool, so distant——' His laughter was rough and shaken, seeming to stab at Liz like a reproach. 'I had one hell of a lot of cold showers that month—but that last night I just couldn't handle it any more. But, Beth, I never——'

'I know.' Liz couldn't bear to hear him repeat her own thoughtless accusation of rape. Even when she'd said it she'd known that it hadn't been true but a deliberate attempt to hurt. 'I *know*. You were trying to reach me— to give—and I saw it as taking.'

'I was desperately ashamed of myself the next day— I always thought I had more control than that. But from the way you responded to me I thought that perhaps, after all, everything was going to be all right, that we'd be able to start again. If only you knew how hard it was for me to go into work the next morning and leave you there. But you were still asleep, and I'd woken so late that I barely had time to get to the office as it was. I told myself that it would only be a few hours before we were together again. I tried to phone several times but there was no answer so I assumed you'd gone into work after all.'

Determined to pack and get away as quickly as possible, she'd ignored the phone all morning, Liz remembered sadly. How different things might have been if she'd answered it.

'And I went home at lunchtime.' Pain shadowed Richard's face, telling her without words just how he had felt then.

By lunchtime she had already left, was already well on her way to her mother's—and of course her mother had been the worst possible person she could have turned to. Embittered and prejudiced by her own painful experiences, Jane Neal was the last person to try and see the man's point of view, to understand Richard and offer an alternative explanation, as Eleanor had done. If only she'd gone to her sister-in-law then, told her everything instead of simply declaring that their marriage had foundered as a result of irreconcilable difficulties and she didn't want to talk about it.

'I wish I'd waited,' Liz sighed sadly. 'I wish I'd talked to you instead of closing in on myself. I was as bad as you for not communicating, not saying how I felt. Neither of us knew how to give or take. Oh, Richard— all that wasted time!'

Looking into Richard's face, she saw her own distress mirrored there.

'The three months I spent without any contact with you at all were sheer hell. I couldn't find any purpose in life, nothing seemed to matter any more. I did try to phone you almost every day in the first few weeks but your mother always answered and she said that you didn't want to speak to me. I even came to the house a couple of times and she slammed the door in my face.'

Liz started in shock. Her mother had told her the first time Richard had phoned, and then she had agreed that not to speak to him was the best way of handling things. But Jane Neal had never said a word about the other calls or the times Richard had come to the house. She had never realised that her mother had taken things quite that far, and she had taken Richard's apparent silence as another indication of the fact that he didn't care for her at all.

'I didn't know about that,' she said hastily, wanting him to know that she hadn't been part of it. 'Mother must have——'

'Decided to make sure that "that man" never came near her daughter again,' Richard finished for her, but this time that derogatory phrase had none of its earlier impact. 'I suppose I can't really blame her—in her mind all men are tarred with the same brush as your father. If I'd known that she wasn't speaking for you I'd have persisted, but instead I gave up—that was when Eleanor decided to take matters in hand. I never did understand why you agreed to write to me.'

'Neither did I,' Liz admitted, recalling the phone call from her sister-in-law, the way Eleanor had pleaded with her to help, to at least let Richard know that she was alive and well. 'At the time I thought it was just that I'd cared for you once, that we'd parted very badly and I wanted to put that right—that even if we couldn't live together we could still be civilised about things—but even then I was probably deceiving myself. The truth was that I couldn't live without you. Oh, Richard, have we really been given a second chance—can we really start again?'

'I can't think of anything I could ever want more than that—and this time it's going to be so very different.' Very gently Richard drew her towards him again, his eyes deep and dark with love. 'Beth, my darling, I've been all kinds of a blind fool, but never again. I've never really told you how much I love you, but I'm doing so now. You're all the world to me, my love. Without you I don't really exist—I can't function. I love you and I need you, and if you'll come back to me I'll spend the rest of my life telling you—and showing you—just how very much you mean to me.'

'And you to me.' Liz sighed her happiness as his arms enfolded her and she was gathered up against him, his lips coming down on hers in the sweetest, most loving, most wonderful kiss she had ever experienced.

'Perhaps that year apart wasn't totally wasted after all,' Richard said thoughtfully a long time later. 'We fell in love so quickly that we never really had time to get to know each other. Most people do that *before* they marry—we had to do it afterwards.' Suddenly a shudder convulsed his strong body. 'When I think of how close I came to losing you forever—and all because I didn't know how to give——'

'We *both* made that mistake in our different ways,' Liz put in gently. 'But now we'll learn from it—we'll both give and take in the right way in future.' Her glowing eyes lifted to his face, her heart leaping at the understanding and love she saw there. 'And I have so much love to give you, my darling.'

'As I have for you,' Richard responded swiftly. 'And there's something else.' He was hunting for something in his pocket as he spoke. 'No—not a present—the thing I most want to give you is myself—and this——'

He held out his hand, palm upwards, and tears of joy burned in Liz's eyes as she caught the glint of gold and recognised the wedding-ring she had left on the pillow on the day she had fled from their house.

'I've carried this with me everywhere since you went. I wanted to keep one tiny part of you with me all the time—and when you agreed to meet me I prayed that one day I'd have a chance to give it back to you. Will you take it, Beth, and wear it again—take this ring, knowing that it means my heart comes with it?'

'What more could I ask for?' Liz whispered, holding out her hand to him.

The ring slid gently and easily into its proper place on her third finger and through a haze of happiness Liz heard Richard's voice and realised that he was repeating the marriage vows he had made over four years before. Her own voice shaking with emotion, she joined in.

'For richer for poorer, in sickness and in health, to love and to cherish, till death us do part.'

And as the sun finally came out from behind the clouds and sparkled on the river below them Liz knew that this small, private ceremony marked the real start of their marriage, with the promise of a lifetime of giving—and taking—of love ahead of them.

Three women, three loves . . . Haunted by one dark, forbidden secret.

ALIX ATKINSON

Boundaries

Margaret – a corner of her heart would always remain Karl's, but now she had to reveal the secrets of their passion which still had the power to haunt and disturb.

Miriam – the child of that forbidden love, hurt by her mother's little love for her, had been seduced by Israel's magic and the love of a special man.

Hannah – blonde and delicate, was the child of that love and in her blue eyes, Margaret could again see Karl.

It was for the girl's sake that the truth had to be told, for only by confessing the secrets of the past could Margaret give Hannah hope for the future.

W●RLDWIDE

Price: £3.99   Published: April 1991

Available from Boots, Martins, John Menzies, W.H. Smith, Woolworths and other paperback stockists.

Also available from Mills and Boon Reader Service, P.O. Box 236, Thornton Road, Croydon, Surrey CR9 3RU